IMAGES OF THE PREACHER

IN

AFRO-AMERICAN LITERATURE

Walter C. Daniel
University of Missouri-Columbia

i

To my wife, Launa, and the many students
who have taught me
while I tried to teach them.

iii

TABLE OF CONTENTS

PREFACE

This book emerged from a course, "Uses of Religion in Afro-American Literature," that I designed and offered at the Missouri School of Religion, Columbia, Missouri, Winter Semester, 1975-76. Students in that course were enrolled at the Universtiy of Missouri-Columbia and at Columbia College, together with some persons in the city who were interested in the material.

The image of the preacher emerged clearly as the class pursued the syllabus. Zora Neale Hurston's Reverend John Pearson became the favorite by far and led me to plan a manuscript that would present a representative black preacher as he has been projected by Afro-American writers whose works have appeared in print during the better part of the last 100 years.

I make no claims that the image is definitive. It has been extracted from fiction, poetry, and drama written by eight different authors: Paul Laurence Dunbar, James Weldon Johnson, Walter F. White, Langston Hughes, Richard Wright, James Baldwin, and Margaret Walker.

I have included biographical data that should help the reader to place the authors and selections into historical perspective. Suggested Further Readings, a selected bibliography on the history of the black church, should help one to understand the seminal influence of the church in the black American experience.

I want to thank Professor Arvarh E. Strickland, Chairman of the Department of History at the University of Missouri-Columbia, for his counsel and encouragement. He has offered helpful suggestions for its improvement. He and I have team-taught topics courses in English and history

vii

that have used portions of the text of this book.

I am particularly indebted to Victor P. Errante, my editorial assistant, who worked as-siduously with me to prepare the book for pub-lication. Without his careful and patient help, I could not have completed the task.

Walter C. Daniel
Columbia, Missouri
March 1981

CHAPTER 1 . . . . INTRODUCTION

Historians generally agree that the slave population in the United States multiplied rapidly. One authority reported that in 1860 there were 3,954,000 black slaves in the South compared to 385,000 white slaveowners. Recent scholarship about American culture has given significant attention to the lifestyle in the slave community. There an American subculture emerged that underscored the seminal differences between black and white men and women in the United States. If it is true that

> Prince and peasant, merchant and agriculturist, warrior and priest, Africans were swept up into the vortex of the Atlantic slave trade and funneled into the sugar fields, the swampy rice fields, or the cotton plantations of the New World,[1]

one cannot expect to find an American black slave stereotype. The range of components was far too wide for that. A slave-master society, based on color forged a unique caste system. Social tensions generated by that dichotomy permeate the political, economic, legal, and aesthetic fabric of living in the United States. It has been the chief element of Afro-American folklore and the raw material for the conscious literary art of black and white American artists. With the white belles-lettres the product has often been called "local color," even if the picture of the black American and his physical and psychological setting was used for political purposes.

---

[1] James W. Blassingame, The Slave Community: Plantation Life in the Ante-Bellum South (New York, 1972), p. 1.

1

The black slave society captured the interest of the white American most often when white [2]
authors justified slavery or lamented its demise.
Free blacks protested bitterly their second-citi-
zenship status in the North and crusaded for the
abolition of slavery in the South while few other
Americans wrote literature about the nation's
color line. The black press--newspapers and mag-
azines--rose in response to segregation and discrimination based on color. But that conscious
writing was directed toward that minority of
Afro-Americans who could read and could buy papers, journals, and books. What they wrote about
interested white audiences only on occasions.

One icon among Afro-Americans during slavery and since is the black preacher. An interesting parallel lies in a comparison between
tribal religion practiced among many tribes who
lived along the coast of West Africa, and ances-
tral homes of most slaves brought to America,
and the status the preacher achieved and has
maintained among blacks. Priests were paramount
in the tribal society. They "foretold events
and discovered jealousy, theft, and evidence of
poisoning," and in addition to their religious
duties were politicians.[3] They were honored and
revered. The religion American slaves formed
seems to defy simple explanation. Certainly, it
was not a mere copy of the meaning of church to
the white American. Slave masters were not uni-
formly pious. Those who practiced in religious
activities fused their worship with social events.

---

[2]See Hugh M. Gloster, Negro Voices in American Fiction (New York, 1948), Chapter 1, "Back-
grounds of Negro Fiction."

[3]See Mechal Sobel, Trabelin' On: The Slavery Journey to an Afro-Baptist Faith (Newport
Connecticut, 1979), for a Chronological Index to
such church establishment.

Slaves fashioned their church activities along the same lines, even more so; for socializing at the church was surcease from labor on the plantation and akin to festivity.

The rise of the black church is an anomaly in American culture. Its Protestant denominations bore the names of Baptist, Methodist, and Presbyterian; but the institutions varied significantly from their white counterparts. In a society devoid of leisure class institutions-- country clubs, cultural societies, fine arts organizations, political parties--the church serves a multipurpose function. In black America it was in slavery, and is now, the place of worship, the concert hall, the benevolent society, the political platform, and the "sacred space" for the community. Marian Anderson and Leotyne Price, to name two celebrated black concert artists, sang in church choirs in their youth and were "discovered" and encouraged by their church members. NAACP mass meetings were held in churches. Many black educational institutions emerged from church organizations.

It is no wonder, then, that the black preacher became the leader of black society in the United States, not unlike the African tribal priest. He was spiritual leader, counselor, and politician. Unless he was a shrewd administrator and an engaging performer in the religious art of the culture, he did not survive as pastor-leader. His was the one free-standing position in the black community, independent in its administration of its affairs. He was often the only black person with leisure if his congregation were sufficiently financially secure. The church buildings his congregation built are monuments to the strength, the good taste, and the pride of the black American society. Some day, cultural historians will write about some of the excellent structures black congregations built in the North and South.

It is an irony of American history that black Americans built and paid for some of the most impressive examples of ecclesiastical architecture in the United States in the late 19th century. These buildings, and the parishioners who bore their costs on woefully menial wages, represent the amazing strength of the Afro-American community. The African Methodist Church, a major black religious denomination in the United States, rose through an incident that took place in Philadelphia about the same time the nation's Founding Fathers were signing the American Constitution in the same city. Free blacks who had worshipped at St. George's Church moved out of that white church to protest color discrimination they experienced at the time the nation was emphasizing liberty and equality in the City of Brotherly Love. Black church organizations date back to 1858. The first racially separate congregations were established in Virginia, South Carolina, and Georgia. The preacher for these congregations has been a vital part of his community in the black "invisible church" during slavery as it was in the dynamic civil rights movement of Martin Luther King, Jr. and other preachers who led and participated in that protest.

Fictional clergymen from 1900 to 1910 "were generally uneducated emotional exhorters characterized by heavy dialect and lack of refinement and social concern or ideal young ministers, characterized by education, refinement, and social concern," one scholar notes.[4] Black

---

[4] See Ronald Gerald Palosaari, The Image of the Black Minister in Black Novel From Dunbar to Baldwin, (unpublished doctoral dissertation, University of Minnesota, 1970). That scholar concludes that black novelists have rejected the ministry as a distasteful racial role in which the black man in America is so often pushed.

authors have understood the range of images. The
black preacher has served as a frame of reference as he has sought to relate significantly to
his congregation, as in the Paul Laurence Dunbar
works included here. James Weldon Johnson's
preacher is the magician-poet, rendered in the
genre of poetry. Walter White, Field Secretary
for the NAACP at the time he wrote the novel of
his that is used here, used the preacher as a
part of his protest against race hatred in a
Southern town. Zora Neale Hurston brought her
own life, her astute studies in anthropology, and
her irrepressible imagination to John Pearson as
husband and preacher. Langston Hughes found the
Afro-American experience rife with the church and
its preachers, male and female; and Richard
Wright made his preachers confront Communism as
they weighed the merits of conventional Christian "faith" against American pragmatism. James
Baldwin uses the metaphors and the paradigms of
black American religion more fully and more effectively than any other author. His Meridian
Henry in Blues For Mister Charlie plumbs the
depth of the role of the black clergy in the
commitment the private and public demands of a
protean society make on him. And Margaret
Walker's Brother Ezekiel illuminates the role
of the preacher in the slave society in her docu-
mented saga of a black family that extends from
ante-bellum Georgia to the Reconstruction.

Imagination combines with social fact to
create these images of the preacher in Afro-
American literature. Verisimilitude, aesthetic
distance, and all other approaches to literary
studies apply here. The works have been chosen
to represent the major genres of the conscious
artist's craft in literature. Each writer is
important in Afro-American literature. The works'
settings cover more than a century of the black
American experience in churches North and South,
rural and urban.

Further reading in the rise of the black
church and its preacher can be found in the
following related bibliography:

SUGGESTED FURTHER READING

Berlin, Ira. Slaves Without Masters: The Free
     Negro in the Antebellum South. New York,
     1974.
Blassingame, John W. The Slave Community: Plan-
     tation Life in the Antebellum South. New
     York, 1972.
Brooks, Walter H. "The Evolution of the Negro
     Church." Journal of Negro History. January
     1922. pp. 11-22.
----------. "The Priority of the Silver Bluff
     Church and Its Promoters." Journal of
     Negro History. April 1922. pp. 172-196.
Cleage, Albert B. Jr. Black Christian National-
     ism: New Directions for the Black Church.
     New York, 1972.
Cromwell, John W. "The First Negro Churches in
     the District of Columbia." Journal of
     Negro History. January 1922. pp. 64-106.
Coulter, E. Merton. "Henry Turner: Georgia
     Negro Preacher-Politician During the Re-
     construction." Georgia Historical Quarter-
     ly. December 1964. pp. 371-410.

Farley, Ena L. "Methodist and Baptist on the
    Issue of Black Equality in New York, 1865
    to 1868." Journal of Negro History.
    October 1976. pp. 374-392.

Fisher, Miles Mark. "Lott Cary, the Colonizing
    Missionary." Journal of Negro History.
    October 1922. pp. 380-418.

Fordham, Monroe. Major Themes in Northern Black
    Religious Thought, 1800-1860. Hicksville,
    New York, 1975.

Frazier, E. Franklin. The Negro Church in
    America. New York, 1964.

Glennie, Alexander. Sermons Preached on Planta-
    tions to Congregations of Negroes. Charles,
    South Carolina, 1884.

Hamilton, H. Charles. The Black Preacher in
    America. New York, 1972.

Heard, William H. From Slavery to the Bishopric
    in the A.M.E. Church. Arno/New York Times,
    New York, 1969.

Hicks, H. Beecher. Images of the Black Preacher.
    Valley Forge, Pennsylvania, 1972.

Hill, Samuel S. Jr. Southern Churches in Crisis.
    Boston, 1967.

Lincoln, C. Eric. The Black Experience in
    Religion. Garden City, New York, 1974.

----------. Martin Luther King, Jr.: A Profile.
    New York, 1970.

Luckman, Thomas. The Invisible Religion. New
     York, 1967.
Mays, Benjamin E. The Negro's God. Arno/New
     York Times, New York, 1969.
Newman, N. Burkett. Black Apostles: Afro-Ameri-
     can Clergy Confront the Twentieth Century.
     Boston, 1978.
Payne, Daniel A. History of the African Method-
     ist Episcopal Church. Arno/New York Times,
     New York, 1969.
----------. Recollections of Seventy Years.
     Arno/ New York Times, New York, 1969.
Pennington, James C. W. The Fugitive Blacksmith,
     or the History of James C. W. Pennington,
     Pastor of a Presbyterian Church, New York,
     Formerly a Slave in the State of Maryland,
     United States. Westport, Connecticut,1971.
"Pilgrimage to the First Negro Church." Crisis.
     May 1972. pp. 160-161.
Rosenberg, Bruce A. The Art of the American
     Folk Preacher. New York, 1970.
Sobel, Mechal. Trabelin' On: The Slave Journey
     to an Afro-Baptist Faith. Westport,
     Connecticut, 1979.
Washington, Joseph Jr. Black Religion: The Negro
     and Christianity in the United States.
     Boston, 1964.

Weber, Max. The Sociology of Religion, translated by Ephraim Firschoff. Boston, 1963.

Wesley, Charles H. Richard Allen: Apsotle of Freedom. Washington, D.C., 1935.

Woolridge, Nancy Bullock. "The Slave Preacher--Portrait of a Leader." Journal of Negro Education. Winter 1945. pp. 28-37.

CHAPTER 2 . . . . PAUL LAURENCE DUNBAR: Three
                   Preachers in Search of
                   Themselves

To have been born black, and a poet, in the
United States in 1872--was not that ambiguous
at the outset? Jean Wagner asks of Paul Luarence
Dunbar in his Black Poets of the United States.
The answer is yes. In Dunbar, one finds a sensitive youngster who realized some literary
talents in himself in high school and who, upon
graduation from high school in his native Dayton,
Ohio, saw no way to follow his interests in writing. But he did achieve a more than ordinary
measure of literary success. During his brief
lifetime he wrote and published hundreds of
poems, which have served as the basis for most
of his reputation. He also wrote prose fiction,
including four novels and a wide production of
sketches and short stories. He tried his hand
at writing drama, and collaborated with James
Weldon Johnson and his brother, J. Rosamond
Johnson as the three of them, together with
Robert Cole, wrote stage songs for the music
hall theatre. He wrote the book for several
musical comedies. "Clorindy, or the Origin of
the Cakewalk" was performed at the Casino Roof
Garden in New York. Other works of his in the
genre included "Uncle Eph's Christmas" and "In
Dahomey." Dunbar's works chosen for this study
do not contain jokes about the "old colored
preacher." Instead, they present images of the
preacher who searches diligently for the role
he should play in his own setting. Only in one
work--"The Ordeal at Mount Hope"--is the preacher necessarily black. Frederick Brent in the
novel, The Uncalled, examines a problem that
transcends race and enters into the conscience
of a youth who struggles with his call to the
ministry. "The Ordeal at Mount Hope" finds a
young black preacher seeking to reverse the conventional role of the church's ministry and to
add a social role to that community leader's

11

work and perception. "The Fruitful Sleeping of
the Reverend Elisha Edwards" carries the flavor
of the black church and its view of its minister,
but, as with The Uncalled, the image is more
rustic than ethnic, and it is essentially humorous, as is much of Dunbar's poetry.

The Uncalled

This novel is distinctive in Dunbar's fiction for it explores the naturalistic trend in
American literature at the turn of the century.
It is a highly sentimental, uncomplicated story
of a young man who rebels against his foster
mother and his community when they seek to force
him to be a preacher. The plot is naturalistic
in that it employs the controversial subject of
heredity vs. environment. No one calls the tension by that name, but the protagonist, Frederick
Brent, finds himself practically alone in his
battle to reject a life's work someone else has
chosen for him. He rejects the convenient and
self-serving romantic idea that man has little
power to make decisions about his own fate. That
conflict within himself and against the society
in which he is born and lives to young manhood
makes the problem of self-determination harder
by its stubborn claims that Brent, the son of
drunken parents, can never overcome the limits
his heritage places upon what his neighbors
think he can become. Ironically, the community
uses the young Brent to test the validity of its
own religious belief. They believe the young boy
can not overcome his determined fate, but at the
same time, they want to take pride in his accomplishment if he should, by his own ingenuity and
perseverance, reach any worthwhile goals. Dunbar
criticizes the community for its lack of humanity with respect to the developing youth in its
midst. Some persons have considered the novel
an attack on religious bigotry, and it is to some

12

extent. That bigotry is not one denomination's prejudice against another, nor that of the church people against the un-churched. Instead, Dunbar attacks a common religious tradition that he describes in one of his several author's intrusions in the plot such as this one:

> Poor, blind, conceited humanity!
> interpreters of God, indeed! We reduce
> the Deity to vulgar fractions. We place
> our own little ambitions and inclinations
> before a shrine, and label them 'divine
> message.' We set up our Delphian tripod,
> and we are the priests and oracles. We
> despise the plans of Nature's Ruler and
> substitute our own. With our short sight
> we affect to take a comprehensive view of
> eternity. Our horizon is the universe.
> We spy on the Divine and try to surprise
> His secrets, or to speak into His confi-
> dence by stealth. We make God the eternal
> puppet. We measure the infinite with a
> foot-rule.

Few works of American fiction deal with a subject so delicate as that which Dunbar probes in The Uncalled. Certain respect for religion and for implicit understanding about the nation's general concept of the call to the ministry make the subject unique in fiction. It, together with an argument over the respective strength of heredity and environment, presents a unique image of the preacher, viewed from within the heart and mind of the central character, the public and private committment of his foster-mother, and the pressures a community places upon those whose lives it wishes to direct. Moreover, as the plot unfolds, the youth whose fate has become the community's business teaches his detractors a level of humanity their Christianity cannot embrace.

Dexter, Ohio, the fictional setting of the novel, is neither a white nor black community.

Its tensions in the novel rise primarily from a lack of Christian charity, although the women are going through the motions of playing the role of Good Samaritan as the action begins. Margaret Brent is dying, and the women of the neighborhood are discussing the disposition of her 10-year-old boy. The woman is dying from the effects of alcoholism. Her husband has already left town. Everyone knows that while he lived there he was the town drunkard. Each woman considers the responsibility of taking the boy into her home. Everyone except Hester Prime has a legitimate reason for refusing him. Their own families are already more than they can care for. Only Hester, the person least likely to seem an appropriate mother, inasmuch as she is an unmarried woman, agrees to become the foster-mother. She does so because it is her Christian duty, never questioning whether the community is right or wrong in believing the Brents could not possibly produce a son who could amount to very much. Hester becomes, without saying so, the spokesperson in the plot for the powers of environment in shaping the destiny of a person whose heritage is faulty. She plans to provide Fred a healthy, moral environment, and to teach him the Christian virtues of perseverance and the American ethic of hard work. If he should become a successful and respected preacher, her sacrifice for him and her own system of values will be vindicated.

Within the 13 years between Hester's taking Fred into her home and his graduation from high school, the two of them live together peacefully and without conflict. Fred exemplifies a model of morality, industry, and respect. He is offered a clerk's job in a store when he becomes 18. Hester sees the opportunity at this time to try to realize her personal ambition by convincing Fred to become a preacher. He can work in the store and take courses at the local Bible Seminary. Her neighbors believe Hester is high-minded and totally unrealistic to expect Tom

14

Brent's son to become a preacher. His father had been a stone-mason, "when he was anything," one agreed; however, Hester had not been sending Fred to school to learn Latin and Greek and algebra with a view toward becoming a stone-mason. She had what her neighbors called "big notions" in her head when she thought a trade was not good enough for the youth. The community's steadfast belief in the power of heredity over the fate of mankind becomes clear in the novel. Fred Brent was going to the Bible Seminary half day and studying for the ministry, the other woman completely collapsed in her seat, folded her arms, closed her eyes, and wondered what would happen next. "Old Tom, drunken Tom, swearing and raving Tom Brent's boy a preacher." She could not believe it. It was against nature; a panther's cub could not become a lamb; it was downright wicked. The thought was, to her, "ashamin' of the Lord's holy callin' o' the ministry." The neighbor women were equally incensed by Hester's prodding Fred with such plans. They knew he had stated consistently that he preferred to learn a good business, while Hester had claimed no one has the privelege of deciding his own life's work. It was for the Lord to appoint and it was wicked to rebel. A part of one of their arguments included the following passage:

> "I don't know how you can know so much what the Lord means for me to do. I should think He would give His messages to those who are to do the work."

> "That's right, Freddie Brent, sass me, sass me. That's what I've struggled all the best days of my life to raise you fur."

Despite his rebellion, Fred entered the Bible Seminary where he found the word not so bad as he had thought. The spirit of healthy competition there whetted his mind and made him

forget some of his annoyance. He soon became
accustomed to being teased by fellow workers at
the store. Hester's teaching perseverance and
respect for work helped. He became one of the
most promising students at the school, and that
accomplishment brought new complications; for
Dexter retained many traditions of its earlier
days. The church remained a center of the town's
social and public life. Everyone knew about
Fred's standing at the Seminary. His fellow
townsmen anticipated sending a "boy preacher"
and felt their doing so would show them particularly favored in the eyes of God. Fred failed
to cooperate with their aspirations; however.
He refused invitations to talk and "exhort" on
the plea that he wished to be fully prepared for
his work before entering upon it. Some accused
him of cowardice. Others wanted to hear him
preach in order to determine for themselves
whether the Bible Seminary had created an environment that could negate the force of Fred's
heritage. They could not forget and would not
forget he was the son of Tom Brent, the drunkard, and the terrible, unspeakable Margaret.
They could not forget he was born and lived the
first years of his life on Mean Street when it
was "mean street." They shook their heads, saying "What good can come out of Nazareth?" Fred
knew their feelings and he distrusted and resented them for the pressure they placed upon him.
He did not want to be a preacher at all but at
times he prayed to become a great one, just to
convince the old folks he could determine his
own destiny. Taylor, his friend and confidant
at the Seminary, advised Fred to stay in the
Seminary, "go through the discipline, and be a
person." Some of Taylor's words seem to echo
Dunbar's own experiences with his profession:

> When I was at school some fool put it
> into my head that I could write. I hardly
> know how it came about. I began scrib-
> bling of my own accord and for my own
> amusement. Sometimes I showed the things

16

to my friend, who was a fool: he bade me
keep on, saying that I had talent. I
didn't believe it at first. But when a
fellow keeps dinging at another with one
remark, after a while he grows to believe
it, especially when it is pleasant. It
is vastly easy to believe what we want to
believe. So I came to think that I could
write, and my soul was fired with the
ambition to make a name for myself in
literature. When I should have been turning Virgil into English for class-room,
I was turning out more or less deformed
verse of my own, or rapt in the contempla-
tion of some plot for story or play. But
somehow I got through school without a
desided flunk. In the mean time some of
my lines had found their way into print,
and the little cheques I received for them
had set my head buzzing with dreams of
wealth to be made by my pen. If we could
only pass the pitfalls of that dreaming
age of youth, most of us would get along
fairly well in this matter-of-fact old
world.

During the second year of Fred's studies at
the Seminary, Reverend Simpson, his pastor,
found his health would not permit him to preach
for a while. The faculty of the school immediately recommended Fred as supply pastor. He
could not avoid the responsibility, but the
young seminarian believed the community would
never accept him as a spiritual leader. He was
only 20 years old and he was Tom Brent's boy.
But as word of the interim pastorate got around
the community, excitement flourished. Old Dan'l
Hastings, who limped on two canes exclaimed,
tapping on the ground with one of his sticks for
emphasis,

What! that young Brent preachin' in our
church, in our minister's pulpit! It's

a shame--an' he the born son of old Tom
Brent, that all the town knows was the
worst sinner hereabouts. I ain't a-goin'
to go; I ain't a-goin' to go.

But the old codger and most of the parishioners were in the church the following Sunday
morning. Friends, enemies, and the merely curi-
ous filled the seats and blocked the aisles.
Reverend Simpson came to assist with the service.
His daughter Elizabeth was there looking proud
and sitting on the ladies' side of the pulpit.
Hester, now Mrs. Hodges after her marriage, was
in her accustomed place on the ladies side of
the pulpit. She wore new strings on her bonnet
in honor of the occasion. One "unregenerated
wag" in the back of the church pointed Hester
out to a companion and said she looked as if she
would spank the preacher if he did not do well.

Shortly before the service began, Fred entered the side door by the pulpit and took his
seat. He was "scared to death," but his step was
firm. Reverend Simpson called on Dan'l Hastings
to pray. He intoned derisively:

O Lord, let not the rarin' horses of his
youth run away with Thy chariot of eternal
truth. Lord, cool his head and warm his
heart and settle him firm. Grant that he
may fully realize where he's a-standin'
at, an' who he's a-speakin' to. Do Thou
not let him speak, but speak through him,
that Thy gospel may be preached to-day as
Thy prophets of old preached it.

When he rose to meet the people's eyes, his
face was haggard and he felt weak. But unflinch-
ingly, he swept his eyes over the crowd, remembered the year's rejection and recrimination he
had experienced in Dexter, quickly decided to
reject the sermon he had already prepared, and
spoke in a ringing voice, "Judge not, that ye be

18

judged. For with what judgement ye judge, he
shall be judged, and with what mete, it mete,
it shall be measured to you again." He began
to speak deliberately, but as the fire in his
heart came forth he poured forth the message he
wanted to give the community for many years:

"Blinded by our own prejudices, circumscribed by our own ignorance, we dare to
set ourselves up as censors of our fellowmen. Unable to see the whole chain of
life which God has forged, we take a single link and say that it is faulty. Too
narrow to see His broad plan, we take a
patch of it and say, 'This is not good.'
There is one who works even through evil
that good may come, but we take the sin
of our brother, and, without seeing or
knowing what went before it or shall come
after, condemn him. What false, blind,
petty judges you are! You women who are
condemning your fallen sisters, you men
who are execrating your sinful brothers,
if Christ to-day were to command, 'Let
him who is without sin cast the first
stone,' look into your own hearts and
answer me, how many of you would dare to
lift a hand? How many of you have taken
the beam out of your own eye before at-
tempting to pluck the mote out of your
brother's? O ye pharisaical ones, who
stand in the public places and thank
God that you are not as other men, beware,
beware. The condemnation that surely and
inevitably shall fall upon you is not the
judgement of Jesus Christ. It is not the
sentence of the Father. It is your own
self-condemnation, without charity, without forebearance, without love; 'for with
what judgement ye judge ye shall be
judged.'"

He continued in that vein laughing the con-

gregation into the self-insight which would
cause them to stop trying to steal the prerog-
ative of heaven; to judge not; for God only is
just. When the sermon was over, the silence was
intense. His eyes looked before him as if he
were looking into the future. His hands were
uplifted as if he would call upon the congregation the very judgement which he predicted.
While the echo of his words still rang throughout the church, he sat down and no one moved or
spoke for an instant. Old Daniel Hastings let
his cane fall upon the floor and some of the
women cried out. Reverend Simpson suddenly remembered to pray and the gossips forgot to whisper when their heads were bowed. There were
some pale faces in the crowd, and some whose
tears had made their eyes red. Few remained behind to shake the preacher's hand. As soon as
the benediction was over, Fred hurried out a
side door and before anyone could stop him, he
was on his way home. Hester accepted all of the
congratulations with complacent condescension.
In a letter to his friend, Taylor, Brent wrote
that he thought he lost his head; the sermon
seemed "sordid and sickening and theatrical."
He reported that although it was extremely well-
received, he had not preached another and hoped
he would not have to do so for that one sermon
had forged a chain which held him in a position
he hated. That was a public declaration that he
is or means to be a preacher. "Do you know, I
feel myself to be an arrant coward," Brent wrote.
"If I had half the strength that you have, I
should have been out of it long ago; but the
habit of obedience grows strong upon a man."

When the church conference met at Dexter
that year, its members and the faculty of the
Seminary agreed that Brent should stand for ordination. He was among ten students who presented themselves for examination. Dunbar wrote
that as the essential questions came to Fred,
"his tongue seemed to move of its own volition

without command from the brain and the murmurs of approval told him he was answering right." He was assigned his hometown parish as replacement for the ailing Reverend Simpson.

His position was not easy for a young man. He had to conduct pastoral visits; to console old ladies who thought a preacher had nothing else to do but listen to them recite their ailments; he had to pray with poor and stricken families whose conditions reminded him of what his own must have been as a young child; and he had to admonish girls nearly his own age who giggled in his face. He wrote to his friend, "I am fairly harnessed now, and at work, although the pulling is somewhat hard, I know my way." And he noted that it is wonderful how soon a man falls into the "cant of his position and learns to dole out the cut-and-dried phrases of ministerial talk like a sort of spiritual phonograph."

His church prospered as the congregation increased in number and people said Fred was a good preacher. Having established himself in his profession, notwithstanding his unwillingness to answer the call to the ministry, Fred considered setting the date for his marriage to Elizabeth Simpson and settling down as pastor of the Methodist church. But his professional and personal crisis came during the second year of his pastorate when Reverend Simpson came to remind Brent that Sophy Davis, a young woman in the community, must be held up to ridicule because of immoral behavior. The old minister said Fred had a good chance for giving the devil in that particular part of the "moral vineyard a hard blow." Fred resisted. "If there is such an example furnished, the people will see it for themselves, and I should be doing a thankless task to point it out to them," he explained. Simpson called this the way the new "mild-and-water style of preaching" that would not work in Dexter. He advised Brent to hold Sophy "up in church" next

Sunday as a fearful example of evil doing.
Still, Brent argued that there were enough texts
in the Bible to cite for moral teaching without
holding up a poor weak moral to curiosity, scorn,
and derision of her equally weak fellows. Simpson
countered by telling Brent he could not fail to
perform his duty as a Christian and a preacher
of the gospel unless he held the woman up to
public scorn. The argument between the two
preachers shows the sharp contrast in their respective attitudes toward Christianity:

> "I do not need to kick a falling girl to
> find examples to warn people from sin;
> and as for duty, I think that each man
> best knows his own."

> "Then you aren't going to do it?"

> "No," the young man burst forth. "I am
> a preacher of the gospel, not a clerical
> gossip."

> "Do you mean that I am a gossip?"

> "I was not thinking of you."

> "Let me preach for you, Sunday."

> "I will not do that either. I will not
> let my pulpit be debased by anything
> which I consider so low as this business."

> "You will not take advice, then?"

> "Not such as that."

> "Be careful, Frederick Brent. I gave you
> that pulpit, and I can take it away,--I
> that know who you are and what you come
> from."

> "The whole town knows what you know, so

I do not care for that. As for taking
my pulpit from me, you may do that when
you please. You put it upon me by force,
and by force you may take it; but while
I am pastor there I shall use my discre-
tion in all matters of this kind."

"Sophy's been mighty quiet in her devil-
ment. She doesn't accuse anybody. Maybe you've got more than one reason for
shielding her."

Brent looked into the man's eyes and
read his meaning; then he arose abruptly
and opened the door.

"I'm not accusing--"

"Go," said the young man hoarsely. His
face was white, and his teeth were hard
set.

"You'll learn some respect for your elders yet, if--"

"Go!" Brent repeated, and he took a step
toward his visitor. Mr. Simpson looked
startled for a moment, but he glanced back
into the young man's face and then passed
hurriedly out of the room.

Brent let two words slip between his
clenched teeth: "The hound!"

Ironically, the young minister whose heritage did not qualify him for his profession in
the eyes of most of the people who lived in Dexter came closer to the essence of Christianity
than his elder in the ministry, the Reverend
Mister Simpson. But their confrontation led to
a quickly called conference of the congregation.
Lay members interrupted the personal conflict between the two ministers. Before they could take

23

official action with respect to Brent's pastorate, the young man addressed them:

> To-night I feel for the first time that
> I am myself. I give you back gladly what
> you have given me. I am no longer your
> pastor. We are well quit. Even while
> I have preached to you, I have seen in
> your hearts your scorn and your distrust,
> and I have hated you in secret. But I
> throw off the cloak. I remove the dis-
> guise. Here I stand stripped of every-
> thing save the fact that I am a man; and
> I despise you openly. Yes, old Tom,
> drunken Tom Brent's son despises you.
> Go home. Go home. There may be work for
> your stench-filled nostrils there.

Brent did not return to the church nor to
the profession of the ministry. He moved away
from Dexter.

The Uncalled abounds in contrivance and
sentimentality as it reflects characteristics of
the Victorian novel in England and in the United
States. It explores the questions of heredity
vs. environment, and of the priority of Christian
duty. By juxtaposing the young, reluctant preacher with the conventional spiritual leader he re-
places breifly, Dunbar portrays images of two
preachers--Simpson's strict pietism and Brent's
humanity. A major irony lies in Brent's character as the sensitive young man who understands
Christianity better than do those who teach it
to him. Simpson might very well have served as
his role model, but Brent's own honesty and in-
dependence point toward an enlightened ministry.
The image has been created through social consciousness the young preacher possesses. He is
the sympathetic protagonist. One sees him as
a prescription for the preacher of the future.
The conclusion of this part of the plot leaves
the question of the meaning of the term "uncalled."

24

Is a Frederick Brent unsuited for the role his community expects of its preacher? The "crisis of conscience" he faces and solves to his satisfaction transcends the limits of any particular ethnic group.

"The Ordeal at Mount Hope"

The name of the community in which young Reverend Howard Dokesbury has accepted a pastorate carries with it an irony. For Mount Hope, by its appearance when the minister descended from the jim-crow coach of the train upon the rotten planks of the station platform, suggested anything but Hope. "And this is Mount," Dokesbury mused to himself. It was hardly inspiring but it was his field of labor. The incompatibility between him and the community was clear. He was handsome and impressive; "the deep, dark brown of his skin, the rich overfullness of his lips, and the close curl of his short black hair" indicated he was a full-blooded Negro and a finely proportioned, stalwart looking youth with a general air of self-possession and self-sufficiency in his demeanor. There was firmness in the set of his lips. His appearance and fine character had prompted authorities at the little college where he had taken his theological training to urge him to go among his people of the South in order to exert his powers and talents for good where the field was broad and the laborers were few. From his Southern parents he had learned many of the traditions and superstitions of the South, but Howard had never been below the Mason-Dixon Line. Yet, with "a confidence born of youth and consciousness of the personal power," he started South with the appropriate skills needed to cope with their shortcomings. He was the new breed of the rural black preacher--committed, vigorous, idealistic, educated and humane. As a radical departure from the conventional preacher, he fostered a new model of black leadership. Because he was a

preacher, he could use the status of that profession to significantly affect the whole quality of life in his station.

   While he is being conveyed to his lodging
place, Dokesbury learns some social dimensions
of his parish. The men made their living at
menial jobs--sawing wood, raising a garden, and
fishing. Their earning power was meager but
their aspirations were also low. They were satisfied with something to eat and drink, clothes
to wear and some place to stay. Given his own
appreciation for an enriched human spirit beyond
mere creature comforts, the young preacher quickly came to believe Mount Hope was, indeed, vir-
gin soil for his ministerial labors. The name
of the place was a double entendre for the story.
The image of the preacher in the sketch emanates
from the confrontation between the bleakness of
the community--in material, spirit, and morali-
ty--and the minesterial passion of the young,
capable, attractive Dokesbury.

   Mr. and Mrs. Stephen Gray, his landlords,
were as poor as their neighbors, but Mrs. Gray
possessed the traditional kindness and warmth
that is associated with the black American family. She tried to make the minister feel at home
as a roomer in her house, but her husband was
at first uncommunicative, responding in gruff,
monosyllabic rejoinders to whatever Dokesbury
said to him that first evening. By bedtime, the
new minister had learned the couple's son Lias
was not, as they said, "what we want him to be."
He was not bad, just careless, they explained,
and asked the preacher to remember their son in
his prayers. As they spoke haltingly of Lias,
Dokesbury felf the old woman's pleading look and
the husband's intense gaze upon his face and suddenly he felt an intimate sympathy for them. He
also realized their dilemma could provide a way
for him to begin the essential part of his ministry his first night in Mount Hope. "There is

no better time than now," he said, "to take his case to the Almighty Power; let us pray." No doubt he had prayed the same prayer many times before and had certainly heard others use the words of supplication and the pleas for light and guidance. But to the young man kneeling there among those humble surroundings, with the sorrow of those poor, ignorant people weighing upon his heart, his role became extraordinary. The words of the prayer came more fervently from his lips and they held deep meaning for him. When he arose there was a radiance in his heart such as he had never before experienced. Mrs. Gray blundered up from her knees wiping her eyes and reciting that Bible verse that promised those who mourn shall be comforted. Her husband shook the preacher's hand warmly and in silence. There was moisture in the old eyes that told Dokesbury his prayer had sounded the proper depths with the Grays.

As he sat in his room to assess the meaning of his first few hours in Mount Hope, Howard Dokesbury had to question his calling. He wondered whether he knew his own people and their aspirations. Was it possible that they could be so different from what he had seen and known? He had not always been such a loyal Negro, so proud of his own brown skin. But had he been mistaken? he asked himself. Was he, after all, different from the majority of the people with whom he was supposed to have all thoughts, feeling and emotions in common? Dunbar describes part of the introspection:

> There was moments when he felt, as every man, howsoever brave, must feel at times, that he would like to shift all his responsibilities and go away from the place that seemed destined to tax his powers beyond their capabilities of endurance. What could he do for the inhabitants of Mount Hope? What was required of him to do? Ever through his mind ran the world-

old question: 'Am I my brother's keeper?'
He had never asked, 'are these people my
brothers?'

Next morning as he walked about the town,
it became clear that perhaps he did not belong in
Mount Hope. People he met viewed him suspicious-
ly or contemptuously--white and black. He felt
alone and helpless. Squalor and shiftlessness,
all about him, depressed him. Children who
should have been playing childhood games were
shooting craps and violently arguing over their
penny wagers. Glib profanity rolled from lips he
thought should be stumbling through catechisms.
He felt estranged from these dispirited people,
but his heart also ached for them.

A disturbance attracted his attention.
There, almost in the path of his journey, Lias
was thrown out of a saloon. Instinctively,
Dokesbury sheltered the boy from an assailant.
Looking in Lias' face, the young preacher agreed
with what Mrs. Gray had told him the night before: Lias might be careless, but he wasn't a
bad boy; for his face was too open and his eyes
too honest for that. No, he wasn't bad, but environment could make him bad. Here was work for
any pastor. And it is this incident that gener-
ates the image of the preacher in the story.

"You'll walk on home with me, Lias, won't
you?" Dokesbury asked. Lias said he might as
well although he did not stay around home as much
as maybe he should. That admission provided an
opportunity for alliance between the minister and
the Gray youth. "It will be so much less lonesome for two people than for one," Dokesbury explained, and, "Then you can be a great help to
me." Lias doubted whether he would be much help
to anyone, especially the preacher, inasmuch as
he had never got religion and wasn't very learned. "Oh, there are a thousand ways in which you
can help, and I am sure that you will," the

pastor assured Gray and got from him the promise he would do the best he could. Lias refused stoutly to go to the mourner's bench, though. But that was not what Dokesbury was going to ask him to do. "What I want is that you will take me fishing as soon as you can. I never get tired of fishing and I am anxious to go here. Tom Scott says you fish a great deal about here."

The elder Gray was pleased to note the growing friendship between his son and the minister. By the end of the first week, the family had grown close. Saturday came and the son was anxious to return to his friends at the saloon. Dokesbury did not try to keep him from going.

Sunday morning, Mr. and Mrs. Gray walked to church with the new pastor. The "pillars of the church" sat in their places looking stern, grim, and critical. Opposite them and like them, in seats at right angles from the main body, sat the older sisters, some dressed with good, old-fashioned simplicity, others gaudily. A dozen or so beribboned mulatto girls sat toward the rear giggling and tittering and casting bold glances at the handsome young minister. After the prayer and in the midst of the second hymn a more pronounced titter from the back seats attracted Dokesbury's attention. He raised his head and looked to see Lias enter the church, obviously drunk as he staggered up the aisle to a seat. His mother wiped her eyes. His father sat with his gaze upon the floor as lines of sorrow surrounded his mouth. Dokesbury reacted differently:

All of a sudden a great revulsion of feeling came over Dokesbury. Trembling, he rose and opened the Bible. There lay his sermon, polished and perfected. The opening lines seemed to him like glints from a bright cold crystal. What had he to say to these people, when the full realization of human sorrow and care and

of human degradation had just come to
him? What had they to do with first-
lies and secondlies, with premises and
conclusions? What they wanted was a
strong hand to help them over the hard
places of life and a loud voice to cheer
them through the dark. He closed the
book again upon his precious sermon. A
something new had been born in his heart.
He let his glance rest for another instant
on the mother's pained face and the
father's bowed form, and then turning to
the congregation began, "Come unto me,
all ye that labor and are heavy laden,
and I will give you rest. Take my yoke
upon you, and learn of me: for I am
meek and lowly in heart: and ye shall
find rest unto your souls." Out of the
fullness of his heart he spoke to them.
Their great need informed his utterance.
He forgot his carefully turned sentences
and perfectly rounded periods. He forgot
all save that here was the well-being of
a community put into his hands whose real
condition he had not even suspected until
now. The situation wrought him up. His
words went forth like winged fire, and the
emotional people were moved beyond control.
They shouted, and clapped their hands, and
praised the Lord loudly.

At the end of the service, all the congregation gathered around the young preacher, shaking his hand and congratulating him upon his sermon. Lias slept through it all. When his mother started toward him, the young minister whispered to her, "Leave him to me." Dokesbury shook
the boy awake with, "Come, my boy, let's go home."
Arm in arm they went out into the street where a
number of scoffers had gathered to laugh at the
abashed boy. But the young minister's strong
arm steadied his step and something in his face
checked the cowards' hilarity. Silently, they
cleared the way and the two passed among them and

went home. In that dramatic experience, the
minister saw clearly the things which he had to
combat in the community and through this one victim he determined to fight the general evil. The
people with whom he had to deal were children
who must be led by the hand. The boy lying in
drunken sleep upon his bed was no worse than the
rest of them. He was an epitomy of the evil as
his parents were the sorrow of the place. But
the remedy did not lie in talking to Lias. He
could not lecture him. He would only be dashing
his words against the accumulated evil of years
of bondage as the ripples of the summer sun beat
against a stone wall. In reality, it was not the
wickedness of this boy that he was fighting, instead it was the aggregation of the evils of the
fathers, the grandfathers, the masters and mis-
tresses of these people. Against this, what
could possibly prevail?

Before long, the Reverend Mister Dokesbury
had encouraged Lias and his shiftless friends to
take the large plot of ground behind the family
house and develop it into a small chicken farm.
The boys built the necessary buildings and were
proud to take care of the chickens and the eggs
and to share the profits. Lias was skilled with
carpentry tools.

One of the boys learned carpentry well enough
to repair houses around the town; another en-
larged the small chicken farm; and still another
had opened a store to sell the fish which the
men around the community caught and brought to
him. Mount Hope had at last awakened. Something
had come to the town to which its people could
aspire--something that they could understand and
reach. True enough, they were not soaring but
they were rising far above the degradation which
was theirs when Howard Dokesbury had first arrived there. Most importantly for Mount Hope and
for the young minister, the ordeal had passed.

The simple, uncomplicated story told perhaps too directly to appeal to literary artists captures the essence of the need for a preacher toward the close of the 19th century in the South where the end of slavery had not brought the freedom it promised. Instead, there had come in its place a kind of moral and economic degeneracy which in many ways was little better than physical slavery. Clearly, the role of the black minister in such a setting--especially one who had received college and theological school training--was to enrichen the lives of the persons with whom he worked. His particular calling provided unusual opportunities for him to provide directions of growth and opportunities to reclaim self esteem which would provide role models for the young persons who could become productive citizens, even in a most unpleasant surrounding.

This particular image of the preacher is one of Dunbar's warmest pieces of fiction. It is simplistic and studiously follows Booker T. Washington's philosophy that properly motivated preachers and teachers could teach industry, piety, and self-esteem to the most destitute community of black Americans.

"The Fruitful Sleeping of the Reverend Elisha
        Edwards"

The preacher in this short story possesses a unique sagacity what leads to his self-preservation. Moreover, the sketch suggests the narrow expectations that a congregation holds for its minister, one that excludes the broad social good we have seen in the understandings of the young Reverend Dokesbury. The story is hardly philosophical; it exemplifies Dunbar's reputation for illustrating rural humor, especially that which surrounded the church. Again, the preacher could be black or white. This lack of ethnic specificity shows levels of understanding about the rural society and its relationship to the minister in its midst as has been seen in the other works.

There was great commotion in Zion Church. For the last six months trouble had been brewing between the congregation and the pastor who had come to them just two years earlier and who had given good satisfaction in his preaching and pastoral work. Only one thing had displeased his congregation, and that was the Reverend Elisha Edwards' tendency toward moments of "meditative abstraction in the pulpit." He could introduce a guest preacher with fiery enthusiasm, and he could "sanction" any pulpiteer during a sermon. But as soon as he began his discourse, Edwards sat in the pulpit with his head bowed and his eyes closed. Some members thought this was a sign of deep thinking or silent prayer and meditation. Others thought the pastor was jealous or indifferent to other preachers who shared his pulpit; so he attempted to ignore them by bowing his head and closing his eyes. One day while Uncle Isham Dyer was exhorting the congregation on the wings of his eloquence and was painting hell for sinners in the most terrible colors when to the utter surprise of the whole audience, a loud and penetrating snore broke loose from the throat of the pastor which,

> . . . rumbled down the silence and startled the congregation into sudden and indignant life like the surprising cannon of an invading host. Horror-stricken eyes looked into each other, hands were thrown into the air, and heavy lips made round O's of surprise and anger. This was his meditation. The Reverend Elisha was asleep!

Uncle Isham turned around and looked down on his pastor in disgust and then returned to his exhortations. But he was disconcerted and soon ended his discourse. As for the pastor himself, his snore rumbled on through the church, his head drooped lower until, with a jerk, he awakened himself. He sighed religiously, patted his foot upon the floor, rubbed his hands together and looked complacently over the agrieved congregation. Some of the old ladies and old men mourned. But the pastor did not know what they had discovered and he simply shouted "Amen" because he thought something Dyer had said was affecting them. When he rose to comment on the local preacher's exhortation, he was strong, fiery and eloquent. But it was of no use. Not a member cried out; no one moaned. Not an "Amen" came from his congregation. Reverend Edwards could not understand this unresponsiveness. The congregation had always responded favorably to him in the midst of his sermons, so he paused to break into a song in order that they would join him again. But this day he sang alone and ominous glances were flashed from pew to pew and from aisle to pulpit. Even the collection was especially small. No one asked the minister home for dinner that day, so he went his way puzzled and wondering.

Before the services the next Sunday, certain members of the congregation met together for a conference. It was the local exhorter from the morning service who opened the proceedings by telling his brothers and sisters that the Lord had opened their eyes to wickedness in high places. He had permitted them to see the man they had trusted with the guidance of his flock asleep in the hour of duty and they should feel agrieved. The members agreed that he surely was asleep and there was no way to dispute that. "I can testify to it," said one sister. She told the others she plainly heard him snore and she actually saw him when he awoke himself with his own snoring. Brother Isham Dyer commented that all the time Reverend Edwards had been sleeping the church had been giving him praise for his meditation. As the stormy meeting continued,

accusation and anger against the minister grew.
Some suggested dismissing him on the spot but
calmer heads prevailed and it was decided to
give him another trial. He was a good preacher,
they had to admit. He had visited them when they
were sick and had brought sympathy to their af-
flictions and a genial presence when they were
well. They would not throw him over without
giving him a last chance to vindicate himself.
One member felt so strongly about the last chance
which the preacher should have that she crept out
of the church and hastened toward the parsonage.
She met the preacher coming to church with his
hymn book in his hand and his Bible under his
arm. She caught him by the arm and told him what
was going on in the meeting. The minister staggered under the blow as he heard what his congregation had been saying. For to leave Zion Church
would be very hard for him. Especially to leave
there in disgrace. Where would he go? His career would be ruined. The story would go to
every church in the connection and he would be
an outcast from his cloth and his kind. Somehow
it all seemed like a mistake. He loved his work
and he loved his people. He wanted to do the
right thing but sometimes the chapel was so hot
and the hours so long. At those times his head
would grow heavy and his eyes would close. But
it had only been for a minute or two. Just this
morning he remembered how he had tried to shake
himself awake, how gradually the feeling had come
over him. And then he had snored. He had indeed not intended to deceive them, but the Bible
had said, "Let not the right hand know why the
left doeth." He did not think it was necessary
to tell them that he dropped into an occasional
nap in church. Now, however, they all knew he
was greatly embarrassed and troubled. Thanking
the woman who had told him what was going on, he
decided he would go back into the parsonage and
pray over the subject.

When he came back into the church that night,

the Reverend Elisha walked with a new spirit, with a smile on his lips and a light of triumph in his eyes. Throughout the long prayer which the deacon prayed early in the service, the pastor's loud and insistent "Amens" kept him awake. His sermon was a masterpiece of fiery eloquence, and as Sister Green stepped out of the church door that night, she remarked that if Brother Edwards was asleep that morning he certainly preached a waking up sermon that night. The congregation hardly remembered that their pastor had ever been asleep. But the pastor himself knew when the first flush of enthusiasm was over that their minds would revert to the crime of the morning which should again vindicate him in the eyes of his congregation.

That Sunday, when he came into the pulpit, their eyes were fastened upon him with suspicious glances as he had expected. Uncle Isham Dyer had a smile of triumph on his face because the day was a particularly hot and drowsy one. And the local exhorter thought he would get his chance to be called as pastor to the church. The Reverend Elisha asked Dyer to say a few words at the opening of the meeting and when the exhorter had scarcely been talking for five minutes the watchful congregation saw the pastor's head droop and his eyes close. For the next 15 minutes little or no attention was paid to Brother Dyer's exhortation. The angry people were nudging one another whispering, and casting indignant glances at the sleeping pastor. He awoke and sat up, just as the exhorter was finishing a fiery period. If those who were watching him were expecting to see any embarrassed look on his face they were mistaken. For instead, his appearance was one of sudden alertness, and his gaze that of a man in extreme exaltation. One would have said that it had been given to him as to the inspired prophets of old to see and hear things far and beyond the kin of ordinary mortals.

As Dyer sat down, the Reverend Elisha Edwards rose quickly and went forth to the front of the pulpit with a firm step. Still, with the look of exaltation on nis face, he announced his text, "If he sleep he shall do well." And then, to the alert attention of his congregation, he spoke first of the benefits of sleep, what it does for the warm human body and the weary human soul. Turning off into a half-humorous, half quizzical strain which was often in his sermons, he spoke of how many times he had to forgive some of those who sat before him today for nodding in their pews. And, raising his voice like a good preacher, he came back to his text exclaiming, 'But if he sleep, he shall do well." He told of Jacob's sleep, and how at night, in the midst of his slumbers the visions of angels had come to him, and that he had left a testimony behind him that was still a comfort to the hearts of all. He lowered his voice and said:

> You all condemns a man when you sees
> him asleep, not knowin' what visions is
> a-goin' thoo his mind, nor what feelins'
> is a-goin' thoo his heart. You ain't
> conside'in that mebbe he's a-doin' mo'
> in soul wo'k when he's asleep then when
> he's awake. Mebbe he sleep, we'n you
> think he ought to be up an' erbout.
> Mebbe he no' an' mebbe he sno't, but I'm
> a-hyeah to tell you, in de wo'ds of the
> Book, that they ain't no 'sputin' 'Ef he
> sleep, he shell do well!'

The church was in smiles of joy as the congregation rocked to and fro from the ecstasy of his sermon. But the Reverend Elisha had not yet placed the cap on his remarks He asked his members to hold on before they would shout and give their sanctions. Did they think that right before their eyes he had gone from meditation into slumber and if so, for what reason? Did they believe he was shirking or lazy? Shouts of "No!

No!" came from the congregation. "No, no,"
agreed the preacher, "I wasn't shirking nor was
I lazy." The soul within him was working with
the mind and he had forgotten his old body. With
his head laid on his breast and his eyes closed,
he could see visions of another day to come. He
could see visions of a new heaven and earth,
when all the people shall be clothed in white
raiment and shall play harps of gold and walk
the golden streets of Jerusalem. That was what
was running through his mind, he told them, when
he sat in the pulpit and seemed to be asleep.
And he asked if they thought it was sinning.

He ended his sermon amidst the smiles and
nods and tears of his congregation. No one had
a harsh word for him now and even brother Dyer
wiped his eyes and whispered to his next neighbor, that Reverend Edwards surely did sleep to
some purpose. The congregation thronged around
the minister as he came down from the pulpit and
held his hand as they had done before. One old
woman went out still mumbling under her breath,
"Sleep on, Edwards, sleep on."

"The Fruitful Sleeping of Reverend Elisha
Edwards" is little more than a humorous sketch
at first sight. But upon closer examination it
indicates how capriciously a church congregation
may regard its pastor and his services. The
image, however, of the preacher in this particular case is encouched in his performance before
his congregation even if that performance is intended primarily for his own self-preservation.
And it captures, at the same time, foibles and
strengths of the rural sense of community that
can destroy or support its leaders. Whether they
will be a positive of negative force often hangs
by a precarious thread. People who know the nature of folk religious practices identify with
the story's properties.

CHAPTER 3 . . . . JAMES WELDON JOHNSON:
"The Turpentined Imagination"

> "The old-time Negro preacher
> loved the sonorous, mouth-
> filling, ear-filling phrase
> because it gratified a high-
> ly developed sense of sound
> and rhythm in himself and
> his hearers."
>
> --Introduction, God's Trombones

James Weldon Johnson (1871-1938) affected the literary and socio-political life of the nation
throughout the first generation of the 20th century. He was an approximation of Renaissance Man,
reaching some accomplishment in journalism, the
diplomatic service, law, education, music, and
literature. Born in Jacksonville, Florida, and
educated at Atlanta University, Johnson became a
public school teacher in his hometown, during
which time he and his brother, John Rosamond
Johnson, wrote "Lift Every Voice and Sing" that
has become known as the "Negro National Anthem."
Some of his well known works include The Autobiography of an Ex-Coloured Man (1912), a novel;
Fifty Years and Other Poems (1917); God's Trombones: Seven Negro Sermons in Verse (1927); and
the satirical long poem, "St. Peter Relates an
Incident" (1935). His autobiography Along This
Way (1933) is an important resource on Afro-
American life, as well as his cultural history
of black New York, Black Manhattan (1930). The
poems in God's Trombones are discussed in study.

39

JAMES WELDON JOHNSON: THE "TURPENTINED IMAGINATION"

GOD'S TROMBONES:
    "Listen, Lord--A Prayer"
    "The Creation"
    "The Prodigal Son"
    "Go Down Death--A Funeral Sermon"
    "Noah Built The Ark"
    "The Crucifixion"
    "Let My People Go"
    "The Judgement Day"

"There is something of wonder in the fact that a quiet little book of some brilliant poems appearing in 1927 was not overlooked," American historian and critic, J. Saunders Redding, writes of James Weldon Johnson's God's Trombones (1927). For, between 1926 and 1935, Afro-American writers became almost obsessed with Harlem as a great urban center. Their representation of life there became a "sort of disease in the American organism"; but Johnson's best known literary work renders into conscious literary from the language and theatrical delivery of the old-time preacher and the compelling genius of that paragon of Afro-American culture. Johnson describes his motivation for writing the poems in the Preface to the collection:

I was speaking on a Sunday in Kansas City, addressing meetings in various colored churches. When I had finished my fourth talk it was after nine o'clock at night, but the committee told me there was still another meeting to address. . . . When we reached the church an "exhorter" was just concluding a dull sermon. After his there were two other short sermons. These sermons proved to be preliminaries, mere curtain-raisers for a famed visiting preacher. At last he arose. He was a dark-brown man, handsome in his gigantic proportions. He appeared to be a bit

self-conscious, perhaps impressed by the
presence of the "distinguished visitor"
on the platform, and started in to preach
a formal sermon from a formal text. The
congregation sat apathetic and dozing.
He sensed that he was losing his audience
and his opportunity. Suddenly he closed
the Bible, stepped out from behind the
pulpit and began to preach. He started
intoning the old folk-sermon that begins
with the creation of the world and ends
with Judgement Day. He was at once a
changed man, free, at ease and masterful.
The change in the congregation was instan-
taneous. An electric current ran through
the crowd. It was in a moment alive and
quivering; and all the while the preacher
held it in the palm of his hand. He was
wonderful in the way he employed his conscious and unconscious art. He strode
the pulpit up and down in what was actually a very rhythmic dance, and he brought
into the play the full gamut of his wonderful voice, a voice--what shall I say?--
not of an organ or a trumpet, but rather
of a trombone, the instrument possessing
above all others the power to express the
wide and varied range of emotions encom-
passed by the human voice--and with greater
amplitude. He intoned, he moaned, he
pleaded--he blared, he crashed, he thundered. I sat fascinated; and more, I was,
perhaps against my will, deeply moved;
the emotional effect upon me was irresist-
ible. Before he had finished I took a
slip of paper and somewhat surreptitiously
jotted down some ideas for the first poem,
"The Creation."

That image of the preacher engaged Johnson's
talents for several years. The masterful character he portrayed in God's Trombones stepped outside the narrow confines of conventional Negro
dialect and achieved high verbal eloquence. He

41

spoke "another language" that rendered the innate
grandiloquence of native African tongues and, at
the same time, related the preacher to his brothers and sisters who shared with him a common racial memory emanating from the American slave experience. He rendered the folk material of his
culture, Johnson wrote, much as John Millington
Synge captured the essence of the Irish pastoral
poetry-makers. The preacher's art was sacred and
secular, employing symbols from within to express
an authentic racial spirit. It transcends the
mere mutilations of English spelling and pronun-
ciation that Johnson had found limiting in much
of his own early poetry and in the popular ver-
nacular of the black American poet. The preacher's sonorous phrases gratified the highly developed sense of sound and rhythm he and his hearers had come to know and admire. His icon dated
back to Colonial days in Afro-American history;
he had, indeed, earned his unique status in the
race Johnson described as "the most priest-gov-
erned group in the country." The preacher's verbal art gave him a large part of his leadership
status. But his breed was rapidly passing, Johnson lamented. "I have tried sincerely to fix
something of him" in the poems, he continued.

"Listen, Lord--A Prayer"

    The first poem in Trombones is a layman's
prayer that employs the poetic diction in the sermons and, in doing so, actually reinforces the
strength of the role of the preacher in the black
folk society. It matches the sonorousness of the
sermons, although any layperson can render it.
The poem begins with a "Collect"--the congregation's prayer for sinner, members and the preacher:

     O Lord, we come this morning
     Knee-bowed and body-bent
     Before thy throne of grace.
     O Lord--this morning--

Bow our hearts beneath our knees,
And our knees in some lonesome valley.

The Lord is entreated to have mercy on proud
and dying sinners, "hanging over the mouth of
hell,/Who seem to love their distance well," and
to "shadow the preacher in the hollow of thy
hand,/And keep him out of the gunshot of the
devil." In a unique mixture of the Roman Catholic
Mass and the daily lives of the Negro slaves, the
prayer asks the Lord to wash the preacher "with
hyssop inside and out,/Hang him up and drain him
dry of sin./Pin his ear to the wisdom-post,/And
make his words sledge hammers of truth--/Beating
on the iron heart of sin." And to "Put his eye
to the telescope of eternity," so he can "look
upon the paper walls of time." From experience of
their daily lives they dredge the idiom as they
ask the Lord to "turpentine" the preacher's imagination and "Put perpetual motion in his arms,/
Fill him full of the dynamite of thy power,/A-
noint him all over with the oil of thy salvation,/
And set his tongue on fire." The speaker speaks
on his own behalf, asking God to remember him
when he has drunk his last cup of sorrow; when he
has been called everything but a child of God;
when he has finished traveling up the rough side
of the mountain; when he starts down the steep
and slippery steps of death. When the world rocks
beneath his feet--then he wants to be lowered to
his grave in peace and await there for the judgement morning. Encrouched in the most dignified
and reverent language a member of the congregation
is capable of expressing, the prayer is one of the
most effective poems of the collection.

"The Creation"

This poem's anthropomorphic God gives the
preacher unlimited license. He can take on the
personna of God, as he uses his physical being and
his voice to recall the creation of the world. It
is the Genesis story at its base, but the preach-

er ascribes loneliness--a human quality--to an omniscient and omnipotent God, conceived in the figure of man: God's creative genius comes in His making the world out of a complete void that extended as "far as the eye could see" in a darkness "blacker than a hundred midnights/Down in a cypress swamp." "Then God smiled," the preacher explained, and "The darkness rolled up on one side,/And the light stood on the other," and, as if good-naturedly practicing His power, God said: "That's good!"

Forsaking the less dramatic Genesis command, "Let there be a firmament in the midst of the waters," the preacher demonstrates an active God in the intimate details of creation:

> Then God reached out and took the light in
>   his hands,
> And God rolled the light around in his
>   hands
> Until he made the sun;
> And he set that sun a-blazing in the
>   heavens.

Again the concrete image of God flinging the dark against the great shining ball, "Spangling the night with the moon and stars," exhibits an active Creator, while at the same time the preacher employs the traditional mystery and power of the story-teller upon his audience. Certainly, bigger than life, God steps down with the sun on his right hand, and the moon on his left, and his extreme supernatural character reflects authenticity. With the stars cluttered about his head and the earth under his feet, God walked, hollowing out valleys and causing mountains to bulge up. When he saw the earth was hot and barren, he "stepped over to the edge of the world/And he spat out the seven seas." The lightning flashed when he batted his eyes, the thunder rolled when he clapped his hand, and the "cooling waters came down."

44

In turn, God created the heavens and the earth,
and all that is within them. But the greatest
marvel of God's creation is man. And quite appropriately, man was created only after God realized: "I'm lonely still." So from the clay which
he had already made in his world, He

Kneeled down in the dust
Toiling over a lump of clay
Till he shaped it in his own image,

He made man, blew his breath into him, and man
became a living soul.

Thus, in a Bible related story, the skill and
the culturally transmitted knowledge of the preacher as story-teller and poet combine with his moral
purpose as religious teacher to capture the imagination of his congregation as he tells once more
the story of the creation of man. Unlike some of
the other sermons this one contains, no allusions
to the social conditions of the Negro in the American setting, nor any direct exhortations to live
the righteous life. Man is God's final and best
creation, partially for two reasons: he was made
to be a companion to God; and he was made in God's
image. If these two implications in the poem are
acceptable, they represent perfectly sound Christian Theology. As poetry--and especially as the
spontaneous poetry of the preacher who speaks
throughout the collection of sermons--"The Creation" represents an ingenious rendering of Christian Theology through its uncomplicated and amaz-
ingly direct manner of raising and answering the
questions concerning man's importance to God.

It is the most popular poem in the Trombones,
not so much because of its simple theology as for
the rapid succession of dramatic action images it
contains. It is a decoration built upon a decoration. It embellishes its Genesis source, and it
fully embodies the vitality of Johnson's black
aesthetic. Its material and feelings come from
"deep within the Negro experience" without a sin-

gle word of dialect that may detract from the seriousness of the preacher's purpose. It illustrates, too, a prime example of a purely American art form as it embraces an alien people's adaptation of an alien religion in which the subjugated people enrich a cultural factor, passed on to them by their captors. It escapes the bounds of a pitiful imitation of the essence of the philosophical heart of Christianity and its language style rescues it from minstrelry. Above all else, it establishes the image of the preacher as the dignified poet-narrator of the collected wisdom of the race.

"The Prodigal Son"

"Young man--/Young man--/Your arm's too short to box with God,: the opening lines of "The Prodigal Son," place this poem outside the legitimate spirit of the old-time Negro preacher. The theme may represent Billy Sunday but not the collected experiences Negro readers would bring to the poem. It is too "worldly" because it refers to boxing, an activity the preacher would not approve for his congregation. Further, although an anthropomorphic God appears throughout Negro folklore, seldom, if ever, does a human being emerge who actually engages in a contest with God. The preacher relates his sermon to the biblical parable simply:

But Jesus spoke in a parable, and he said:
A certain man had two sons.

Without a logical transition from the popular evangelism image of the first stanza, the poem moves quickly through the matter of the inheritance of the two sons as quickly as the original text passes over the elder son's request and the father's agreement. Because the Negro family known to the preacher and his congregation would seldom possess property of any consequence, the poem does not need to labor this part of the narrative.

46

But the preacher does concern himself with a
younger son who leaves home, suggesting the rapid
and consistent displacement of the Negro family
during slavery, Reconstruction, and the migration
North during World War I. Significantly, then,
the poem includes:

    And the father with tears in his eyes said:
        Son,
    Don't leave your father's house.
    But the boy was stubborn in his head,
    And haughty in his heart,
    And he took his share of his father's
        goods,
    And went into far-off country.

Then comes the stanza thich contains the first
interpolation characteristic for this kind of
preaching:

    There comes a time,
    There comes a time
    When ev'ry young man looks out from his
        father's house,
    Longing for that far-off country.

The repetition of the first line represents a
method of emphasis in this art form, and the ob-
servation in the next lines expresses an archetypal human experience; thus both portions of this
short stanza would be sanctioned by the congregation. Because exhortation is the perceived
purpose of the sermon, the preacher becomes more
anxious to foreshadow the end of his story than
does the biblical parable as he instructs his
hearers, again outside the structure of his reference point:

    Smooth and easy is the road
    That leads to hell and destruction.
    Down grade all the way,
    The further you travel, the faster you go.
    No need to trudge and sweat and toil,

Just slip and slide and slip and slide
Till you bang up against hell's iron gate.

As if the moral of the parable may be missed
by his merely telling the story, the preacher rel-
ishes the opportunity to reiterate concrete and
meaningful images in the last line of the passage
quoted above.

The largest portion of the sermon emphasizes
the city to which the young son journeys. It is
"bright in the night-time like day"; its streets
are "all crowded with people"; "Brass bands and
string bands a-playing"; and ev'ry-where the young
man turned/There was singing and laughing and
dancing." When the young man asks the name of the
city, he is told, "This is Babylon, Babylon/That
great city of Babylon." No reference is made to
the Babylon in the biblical parable, but here one
sees at work again a common license practiced in
this folk-art. The choice of the name of the city
is loosely consistent with the connotation of
Babylon elsewhere, but it also gives the preacher
a vocal sound which is at once bombastic and for-
bidding. The exhortation warns

You can never be alone in Babylon,
Alone with your Jesus in Babylon.
You can never find a place, a lonesome place,
A lonesome place to go down on your knees,
And talk with your God, in Babylon,
You're always in a crowd in Babylon.

Most importantly, though, for his own purposes,
the preacher lingers over the sins in Babylon.
The young man "bought himself some brand new
clothes"; "he spent his days in the drinking dens"
and he "spent his nights in the gambling dens";
and he met up with women in Babylon

Dressed in yellow and purple and scarlet,
Loaded with rings and earrings and bracelets,
Their lips like a honeycomb dripping with
    honey,

Perfumed and sweet-smelling like a jasmine
flower;

These women--"sweet-sinning women of Babylon"--
stripped him of his money"; "they stripped him of
his clothes,/And they left him broke and ragged/
In the streets of Babylon."

The biblical prodigal "would fain have filled
his belly with the husks that the swine did eat."
The preacher's young man chose to join the down-
and-outers in Babylon:

Then the young man joined another crowd--
The beggars and lepers of Babylon.
And he went to feeding swine,
And he was hungrier than the hogs;
He got down on his belly in the mire and mud
And ate the husks with the hogs.
And not a hog was too low to turn up his nose
At the man in the mire of Babylon.

In that portion of the poem which tells of the
return of the prodigal son to his father's house,
the preacher omits entirely the reactions of the
older son and the father's sagacity in amelio-
rating the hostility between his two sons, a portion of the parable which is often used by theo-
logians to teach a greater lesson than the mere
return of a "fallen son" to his previous estate.
The preacher's evangelistic purposes seem clear
in the final stanza:

Young man, come away from Babylon,
That hell-border city of Babylon.
Leave the dancing and gambling of Babylon,
The hot-mouthed women of Babylon;
Fall down on your knees,
And say in your heart,
I will arise and go to my Father.

The theme of "The Prodigal Son," accomplishes
Johnson's purposes despite the inappropriateness
of the boxer image. The poem creates preacher,

pulpit, and congregation; thus, it captures the
folk spirit of the poet's subject matter. The
language achieves appropriate dignity, respectable
tinges of human, and the preacher's theological
and social argument. Its base is sufficiently
familiar to the audience; its interpolations a-
bound with local and temporal racial concerns that
the preacher should address as moral teacher. As
a sermon, "The Prodigal Son" parallels the dramatic and didactic purposes the stained-glass windows have in church architecture. It is the message transmitted by an animate medium. In it the
preacher's broad poetic license permits him to
teach by moving from the known (in the case of the
popular biblical parable) to the felt (the life
habits of the wayward community). Through this
honored technique of communication, the preacher
who is the most firmly formed authority in the
Negro culture, gains artistic control for a useful purpose. The irrational structure of his
narrative is sufficiently authentic. It shows
the magical power of the preacher to break through
to any member in the congregation. Both the sinners and the "saved" benefit. The eternal mission
of evangelism may work to a sense of community in
the audience--the sinner becoming the "saved" and
the "saved" rejoicing. The poem, as is true of
all works in God's Trombones, contains no prescribed "answering" from the congregation. But
everyone understands well so popular a religious
subject and the common fables of the "straying"
men of the Christian community--loose women, wine,
dice.

"Go Down Death--A Funeral Sermon"

A people who found solace in anticipating a
"better world" after death, expected the preacher to reassure them that a deceased friend, neighbor, or relative had found relief from sorrow and
deprivation in death; thus, conducting funerals
become a vital responsibility for Johnson's
preacher-poet. No authentic funeral sermon could

50

fail to bring comfort in their bereavement. The
ritual required some recital of the virtues of the
and some exhortation to the community in general
and to any "wayward" family member. Death is the
common plight of mankind, and the church and its
preacher held the responsibility to keep this bio-
logical fact as closely related as possible to the
practice of religion. A funeral was a celebration
of the life of the decedant, but their death, experienced the fortunate fall from the rigors of
mortal life into blissful mortality. The personal
relationship between the Christian and Jesus
Christ provided the rationale for social and religious perposes of the church in the culture--
that those who live the exemplary Christian life
could join the celebrated deceased in heaven after death.

Appropriately, then, the funeral sermon begins:

Weep not, weep not
She is not dead;
She's resting in the bosom of Jesus.
Heart-broken husband--weep no more;
Grief-stricken son--weep no more;
Left-lonesome daughter--weep no more;
She's only just gone home.

The language-making preacher has, at the same
time, brought condolence and reassurance to the
mourners. He has described for the closest relatives their bereavement and with cosmic authority he has pronounced the basic tenet of Christianity. Now he moves into another important element of the funeral sermon. For he must show his
intimate acquaintance with the deceased and his
superior understanding of the mystery of death and
suffering:

Day before yesterday morning
God was looking down from his great,
    high heaven,
Looking down on all his children,
And his eye fell on Sister Caroline,

51

Tossing on her bed of pain
And God's big heart was touched with pity,
With the everlasting pity.

With his eyes upon a full and only vaguely
broken tapestry of the physical as well as the e-
motional relations between God and man and between
earth and heaven, the preacher follows the
Christian conventions of the management of Heaven
in a somewhat military _figura_, with an air of complete understanding:

And God sat back on his throne,
And he commanded that tall, bright angel
    standing at his right hand:
Call me Death!
And the echo sounded down the streets
    of heaven
Till it reached away back to the
    shadowy place,
Where death waits with his pale white
    horses.

In detailed grandeur, the poem relates God's
message to Death to "Go down. . .to Savannah,
Georgia/Down the Yamacraw,/And find Sister Caroline," who has "Borne the burden and the heat of
the day"; who has "labored long in my vinyard"until she is tired and weary; "Go down, Death, and
bring her to me." With a masterful mixture of
stealthiness and obedience, Death rode "Through
heaven's pearly gates,/Past suns and moons and
stars," "And the foam from his horse was like a
comet in the sky," "Leaving the lightning's flash
behind," as he carried out his mission.

The ride of Death from the throne of God--far
into the sky--brings him to Sister Caroline where
"we were watching round her bed." She, unmistak-
enly a good Christian, "turned her eyes and looked away" from her friends and relatives, for "She
saw shat we couldn't see." She was not afraid of
Death; he was to her a welcome friend. So, following the time-honored tradition of the poetic

rendition of the death of a Christian, "she whispered to us: I'm going home,/And she smiled and
closed her eyes."

Death, in this tradition, took Sister Caroline
in his "icy arms,"/But she didn't feel no chill."
She was ready; Death was efficient; so "there he
laid Sister Caroline/On the loving breast of Jesus."

> And Jesus took his own hand and wiped
>   away her tears,
> And he smoothed the furrows from her
>   face,
> And the angels sang a little song,
> And Jesus rocked her in his arms,
> And kept a-saying: Take your rest,
> Take your rest, take your rest.

And the ending, quite appropriately, a refrain:

> Weep not--weep not,
> She is not dead;
> She's resting in the bosom of Jesus.

The treatment of death evades any complex theological thesis. He is like Emily Dickenson's visitor, though courtly in a different manner. Negroes, such as Sister Caroline, worked hard and often became fatally ill. Financially unable to secure good medical treatment, they lingered long in
their miseries and, no doubt, welcomed death. Unlike "The Prodigal Son," though, "Go Down Death"
contains no direct exhortation to the living; yet,
the subtle implication lies strongly as the basis
of the sermon. For, those who hear the sentimental and plaintively tender story of Sister Caroline's death whould emulate her life, so their
death may be like hers.

"Go Down Death" successfully accomplishes the
purposes Johnson intended for these poems. And it
is wholly a creative matter for the preacher

who is being imitated. Its content is not based on a Bible story, so there is little parroting of the King James language mixed with the flavor of Negro folk speech. The preacher has "preached a good funeral"; he has not been "hard on the family"; he has engaged no awkward beginnings or endings; he has said nothing extraneous. The sermon is sheer tenderness as testimony and as folk theology. Its language is dignified and, at the same time, properly sentimental. Its particularization makes it a highly personal eulogy, although its basic form is used frequently enough to represent the funeral sermon at its best in Negro folk-culture.

"Noah Built The Ark"

This poem portrays the preacher in a role different from all the others in Trombones. Here he delivered a postiche of two major Bible stories that provide an acceptable rationale for the purpose of the church and its preacher. Its subject matter lies within the responsibility of the moral teacher, but his own creative genius here illustrates a warmly human quality in one who teaches and entertains as he preaches his art. He borrows a setting from the Fall of Adam to get to The Flood:

> In the cool of the day--
> God was walking--
> Around in the Garden of Eden.
> And except for the beasts, eating in
>   the fields,
> And except for the birds, flying through
>   the trees,
> The garden looked like it was deserted.
> And God called out and said: Adam,
> Adam, where art thou?
> And Adam, with Eve behind his back,
> Came out from where he was hiding.

In these last two lines, the preacher injects

subtle domestic humans. In the second stanza when
God asks Adam who has eaten the fruit of the tree,
the initial, non-verbal response seemed appropriate to an audience that could fully understand the
eternal battle of the sexes the lines suggest:

> And Adam,
> With his head hung down,
> Blamed it on the woman.

Then, the poem goes back to the portion of the
Genesis narrative, not a part of the Noah story:

> Then pretty soon along came Satan.
> Old Satan came like a snake in the grass
> To try out his tricks on the woman.
> I can imagine I can see Old Satan now
> A-sliding up to the woman.
> I imagine the first word Satan said was:
> Eve, You're surely good looking.
> I imagine he brought her a present, too,--
> And if there was such a thing in those
>   ancient days,
> He brought her a looking glass.

Adding the present and the looking glass to
the Bible story teases the congregation. Often
the preacher used asides to illustrate the cunning
of women and the gullibility of men. The license
leads into an exhortation as the preacher moves
back quickly into his conventional role with,
"Don't ever get friendly with Satan." The tempter
is a "con-man," the most successful image of one
who beguiles women, only to lead them and their
spouses to eternal damnation:

> And Satan laughed a devilish little laugh,
> And he said to the woman: God's fooling
>   you, Eve;
> That's the sweetest fruit in the garden.
> I know you can eat that forbidden fruit,
> And I know that you will not die.

And once more, the invitation to laugh easily: "Man first fell by woman--/Lord, and he's doing the same today."

That's how sin got into the world: "From wickedness to wilderness,/Murder and lust and violence,/All kinds of fornications."

By indirection, the preacher has brought his sermon through the Fall of Adam into the presence of Original Sin. That, he said, is the reason God became angry at the sins of men and regretted ever having created him. As the awesome jealous God of the early Old Testament, he says he will destroy man: "I'll bring down judgement on him with a flood,/I'll destroy everything on the face of the earth," except the fishes.

Who, then, can abide the righteous indignation and the cosmic wrath? Only Noah, "a just and righteous man," who walked and talked with God. One day in their conversation, God warns Noah to build an ark:

> Build it for you and all your house,
> And to save the seeds of life on earth;
> For I'm going to send down a mighty flood
> To destroy their wicked world.

The preacher's Noah worked for one-hundred years, while every day "The crowd came round/To make fun of Old Man Noah." They laughed and said: "Tell us, old man/Where do you expect to sail that boat/Up here amongst the hills?" Noah was not deterred from his task by those who mocked him. Once in a while he laid his hammer and saw aside and preached about the coming day of judgement.

Most of the rest of the poem renders the basic plot of the Genesis story--the righteous man who draws into the safety of his ark his own family and one male and one female of all the animals. The church's purpose has been learned as Noah has been held up to the congregation for his piety and

and the rewards he won while the sinners perished. It is a self-rendering recitation that identifies the preacher with the Genesis Noah. The preacher used free humor and unfettered license to fashion an entertaining sermon. Making his own stories from well-known excerpts of biblical narratives known to all his congregation stands as an essential characteristic of Johnson's preacher's art.

"The Crucifixion"

Johnson's poetry accentuates the Afro-American's traditional identification with the suffering servant image of Jesus Christ. Slavery fixed the association so deeply that this metaphor from Christianity dominates the Negro spiritual. Lynching and scourage accorded will with the Crucifixion. Jesus Christ's suffering carried essential meaning for Christianity. Black slaves experienced meaningless suffering, though. Most often it remained unnoticed except by those it touched. Earliest black artistic expression related the ancient Hebrew with the American slave. Johnson marveled at the power of the unlettered, primitive Afro-Americans' rendering into song their American status. In his "O Black and Unknown Bard," one of his earliest poems that expresses an ethno-atheistic, Johnson raised the rhetorical questions: "How in your darkness, did you come to know/The power and beauty of the minstrel's lyre?" To him, these slaves felt "the ancient faith of prophets rise" within their "dark-kept" souls as they burst into "Steal Away to Jesus," "Roll Jordan, Roll," "Swing Low, Sweet Chariot" and the host of spirituals that serve as the linchpin between black America and the Christian religion. Heaven represented surcease from earthly suffering but meaningless suffering--lynching, scourging as the slaves' experience--fostered creative expression. The folk sang the spirituals of their culture and internalized the lyrics; and they also relived the sorrow of the Christ story as a metaphor of their own. That oneness with

Jesus Christ found its capstone in the Crucifixion.

Easter was the principle feast day of the
black church because of the impact of the Cruci-
fixion--not so much the end of Lent or the
Resurrection. The Garden of Gethsemane and Golgotha became Johnson's preacher's chief symbols,
especially as he sensed the tragic aloneness of
Jesus:

>Jesus, my gentle Jesus,
>Walking in the dark of the Garden--
>The Garden of Gethsemane;
>Saying to the three disciples:
>Sorrow is my soul--
>Even unto death;
>Tarry ye here a little while,
>And watch with me.

This is the Jesus Christ stripped of any di-
vinity--alone, afraid, and expecting death. "My
burdened Jesus," the preacher exclaims, as he refers to "The bitter cup"; "Jesus, my sorrowing
Jesus," as "the sweat like drops of blood" formed
on his brow. The only intimation of the compli-
cated theory of the Son of God in Jesus comes when,
in struggling with the pains of his humanity,
Johnson's preacher's Jesus reaches his resolve:
"Not as I will,/Not as I will,/But let Thy will be
done."

The pathetic images of the biblical narrative
combine with the preacher's own unique story:

>Oh, look at black-hearted Judas--
>Sneaking through the dark of the Garden--
>Leading his crucifying mob.
>Oh, God!
>Strike him down!
>Why don't you strike him down,
>Before he plants his traitor's kiss
>Upon my Jesus' cheek?

Having aroused ire in his active and vocal congregation, the preacher returns to the conventional narrative as he takes "my blameless Jesus" through Pilate's court, and the agony of the mob demanding his crucifixion. As he describes the preparation of the crown of thorns, he elicits identification and empathy from his congregation. In the trip up Golgotha's rugged road, he brings the Negro race solidly into an unmistakable oneness with Jesus and his suffering as he intones:

I see him sink beneath the load,
I see my drooping Jesus sink.
And then they laid hold on Simon,
Black Simon, yes, black Simon:
They put the cross on Simon,
And Simon bore the cross

Simon the Cyrenian has long served to relate black Americans to helping bear Jesus' cross.

The audience undergoes the vicarious experience of the agony of being nailed to the cross, the "Roman spear plunged in his side," and weeping Mary who sees her son on the cross, ironically placed between two thieves. The universe became disoriented as the "mid-day sun refused to shine," "Thunder rumbled," and the "unknown language in the sky" wrote: "What a day! Lord, what a day!/ When blessed Jesus died." The witnessing Christian reacted to the cosmic incident. His mystical and personal response became the final verse of the preacher's sermon:

Oh, I tremble, yes, I tremble,
It causes me to tremble, tremble,
    tremble,
When I think how Jesus died;
Died on the steeps of Calvary,
How Jesus died for sinners,
Sinners like you and me.

Here the ever-popular and awesome Negro spiritual "Were You There When They Crucified My Lord?"

clenched the preacher's rendition of the story of
the Crucifixion. From deep within the corporate
experience of suffering in slavery and depriva-
tions after slavery, Johnson's preacher has selected the central Christian touchstone for his
congregation and presented its most pathetic
elements to bring his people an authentic and
essential Christian message. He relates with restraint the black experience to the Crucifixion.
Johnson wrote that this poem was the hardest for
him to write, for its effectiveness depended upon
its simplicity.

Although the Crucifixion lies at the center
of conventional black Christianity, the preacher
of the poem maintains the passive nature of Jesus'
church without the rancor he might have injected
into his portrayal. And he renders his story in
dignified language, choosing for his own use from
among several versions of the Crucifixion that
appear in the Gospels. The poem is at once theological, sociological, and dramatic. It does not
mention the Resurrection, although the sermon is
delivered on Easter Sunday. He has brought to his
congregation a recognizable image of the suffering
Jesus. The eloquent art of the preacher points
toward a religion whose efficacy did not die with
Jesus on the cross.

"Let My People Go"

Understandably, the Exodus story of Moses and
his leadership of Israelites during their bondage
in Europe would capture the interest of the old-
time black preacher. Afro-American life in the
United States paralleled the Hebrew's experience
with slavery, so familiar in the Judeo-Christian
religious tradition. Through the imagination of
their own preachers, American slaves identified
with the captive Hebrews, although they could
hardly consider themselves God's chosen people
historically. The Egyptians and the Hebrews
served different gods, but the Afro-Americans

and their slave masters share the same religion.
The spiritual "Let My People Go" parroted the
Exodus story of the confrontation between Moses
and Pharoah.   Every potential leader among black
Americans--before and after Emancipation--
aroused some promise that he may lead his people
to a "promised land."   The dream of freedom and
the protest against physical slavery and racial
discrimination gave rise to an art form that is
uniquely American.   Through it, Afro-Americans
united their civic and social aspirations to the
fulfillment Christianity offered.

Inasmuch as the preacher became the undisputed
leader of a people whose single free arena of expression he dominated, the preacher was the natural spokesman whose biblical rhetoric could ver-
balize his race's aspiration.   In using the Hebrew
history for his touchstone, the preacher could
maintain the discipline and authority of the
Christian church, legitimize his protest by casting it in the language of the Bible, and, at the
same time, work his own oral magic as living poet.

"Let My People Go" employs an abbreviation of
the essential plot of the ordering of Moses:

Then God again spoke to Moses,
And he spoke in a voice of thunder:
I am the Lord God Almighty,
I am the God of thy fathers,
I am the God of Abraham,
Of Isaac and of Jacob.
And Moses hid his face.
And God said to Moses:
I've seen the awful suffering
Of my people down in Egypt.
I've watched their hard oppressors,
Their overseers and drivers;
The groans of my people have filled my ears
And I can't stand it no longer;
So I'm come down to deliver them
Out of the land of Egypt,
And I will bring them out of the land

61

Into the land of Canaan;
Therefore, Moses, go Down,
Go down into Egypt,
And tell Old Pharoah
To let my people go.

The preacher interposes "overseers" and "drivers" into Moses story to make the Hebrew experience his own. Moses complains that he is a slave of tongue, and God tells him, "I will be thy mouth and I will be thy tongue." In Exodus, the Israelites want permission to go outside Egypt in order to practice their own religion. Johnson's preacher omits this element in the plot. In the American slave's case, though, he and his masters are already brothers in the same religion. The question, then, becomes paradoxical, as the next stanza shows:

And the Pharoah looked at Moses,
He stopped still and looked at Moses;
And he said to Moses: Who is this Lord?
I know all the gods of Egypt,
But I know no God of Israel;
So go back, Moses and tell your God,
I will not let his people go.

The preacher tells his listeners that poor old Pharoah who knows all of the knowledge of Egypt never knew the "one and living God," suggesting that the slave owner, who himself was the Christian and who had taught that religion to his slaves, did not <u>know</u> the "living God" of his own religion.

The long list of plagues the Hebrew God visits upon the intransient Pharoah only hardens his heart. His order to slay the first born of the slaves drives Moses to lead his people out of Egypt, comforted with the promise that God will provide them the protection of a pillar of cloud by day and a pillar of fire by night until they arrive at the Red Sea. At this point in his sermon, the preacher particularizes the unsung slaves'

contribution to the making of America, a cornerstone of the development of the economic fibre of
the nation. He dramatizes the plight of a society
that would find itself bereft of its servants:

> In the morning,
> Oh, in the morning,
> They missed the Hebrew Children.
> Four hundred years,
> Four hundred years
> They'd held them down in Egypt land.
> Held them under the driver's lash,
> Working without money and without price.
> And it might have been Pharoah's wife that
>   said:
> Pharoah--look what you've done.
> You let those Hebrew Children go.
> And who's going to serve us now?
> Who's going to make our bricks and mortar?
> Who's going to plant and plow our corn?
> Who's going to get up in the chill of the
>   morning?
> And who's going to work in the blazing sun?
> Pharoah, tell me that!

Facing the full impact of the loss of his
wageless force, Pharoah gathered his army to pursue the fugitive slaves to the edge of the Red
Sea. There, the dramatic passages about crossing
the sea and the swallowing up of the Egyptians
engages the preacher's strongest rhetoric power.
In the tradition of abolitionist protest, the poem
ends with a direct address:

> Listen!--Listen!
> All you sons of Pharoah.
> Why do you think you can hold God's people
> When the Lord God himself has said,
> Let my people go?

The narrative and the address of the sermon
have come from deep within the black American experience and it has fashioned a useful form from
the ingenious molding of the preacher's art and

63

his imagination with the public authority found in the Christian Church's Bible. Thus, it serves its sacred and secular purposes and retains much of the King James eloquence.

"The Judgement Day"

This poem presents the preacher in his authoritarian personna, as he employs the prophetic revelation of the Christian conception of the end of the world by fire. Without a specific scriptural model, he reminds his congregation of the dual vision of a conception of the end of life: That in addition to the surcease from sorrow which "Go Down, Death" tenderly describes, general judgement on all creatures of earth will be an awful experience. It is the preacher's apocalyptic vision:

> In that great day,
> People,in that great day,
> God's a-going to rain down fire.
> God's a-going to sit in the middle of the air
> To judge the quick and the dead.

And, once again, the all-powerful, God, unquestioned Ruler of the World he has made, will destroy the world. That tall, bright angel, Gabriel, will be called by God to blow his silver trumpet to all the living nations. As God's signal corpsman, he can put one foot on the mountain top and the other in the middle of the sea to blow his trumpet to also wake the nations underground. The first stanzas parallel closely the Negro spiritual, "Fare Thee Well." But the high drama of the poem's narrative carries a vivid picture of the Great Awakening on Judgement Day:

> And I feel Old Earth a-shuddering--
> And I see the graves a-bursting--
> And I hear a sound.
> And what sound is that I hear?
> It's the clicking together of the dry bones,

Bone to bone--the dry bones.
And I see coming out of the bursting graves,
And marching up from the valley of death,
The army of the dead.
And the living and the dead in the twinkling
    of an eye
Are caught up in the middle of the air,
Before God's judgement bar.

This sermon of exhortation turns on how sinners will be able to survive the awesome day.
"Gambling man," "whore-mongering man," "liars and
backsliders" from the conventional catalogue of
the preacher's vilest sinners, as he asked again,
"where will you stand?" For, that day, "God will
divide the sheep from the goats,/The one on the
right hand, the other on the left." Those on the
right will enter into the Kingdom, those who have
"come through great tribulations"; who have
"washed their robes in the blood of the Lamb" will
enter clothed and spotless white, with starry
crowns upon their heads, with silver slippers on
their feet, with harps in their hands:

And two by two they'll walk
Up and down the golden street,
Feasting on milk and honey
Singing new songs of Zion,
Chattering with the angels
All around the Great White Throne.

Those on the left will depart from God into
everlasting darkness, down into the "bottomless
pit," and "the wicked like lumps of lead will
start to fall/Headlong for seven days and nights
they'll fall/Plumb into the big, black, red-mouth
of hell,/Belching out fire and brimstone." Then
it will be too late for sinners to repent. The
planet will disintegrate, and time will become
eternity. With such a fate, surely any sinner
should contemplate the preacher's concluding
question: "Where will you stand/In that great day
when God's a-going to rain down fire?"

65

The preacher has performed his duty in his most effective oratory. His imagery has been striking; his voice has thundered out his most important message as the moral leader of his people; he has authenticated his warning with generous snatches of the King James Bible's language. In his exhortation by question he has kept before his people the final purpose of life, and he has done so with an impressive simplicity, avoiding theological complications. Shorn of any side remarks, the poem remains a "dramatic recitation," but its form and content lie deep within the American black experience and defies, in its own way, any critical analysis that does not bring that experience to a reading of the poem. Its authenticity makes it a good poem in the collection. And still, a reader who approaches it from outside the black American religious experience should recognize in it the mixture of the lore of Christian evangelism seen by the serious and discerning eye of the unlettered but dignified Negro preacher and his understanding congregation. Generous portions of the properties of poetry raise the sermon to an art form which only a conscious artist who respects the folk material and who commands the skill of literary artists could possibly produce. Its humor arises not from any sense of ridicule of the preacher's words of his theology. One who smiles at all as he reads it does so because the poem is to him "almost a memory" or his amused delight at the eloquence. Its drama infects; its measured and studied rhythm issues spontaneously; and its practicality inspires awe. It is the indispensable property of any black preacher who would succeed in the traditional congregation.

Critics have complained that one can hardly tell Johnson from the preacher in God's Trombones. That is a valid criticism, but the poet has clearly set forth his purposes in the introduction to the volume. Add to those aesthetic purposes Johnson's desire to record what was, to him, the vanishing art of the old-time preacher as the poem reflects him, and one becomes less concerned about

the delineation between the poet and the preacher.
They are both poets and they both take license.
No one of the poems--with the possible exception
of "Listen Lord" and "Go Down, Death"--may be considered a complete "recitation" without the rhythm,
the flavor, the fervor, and the celebration which
always have and always will remain a part of the
religious setting in which these folk materials
are appropriate.

The poems, though, taken together, present a
consistent image of the preacher and the work,
itself, holds a secure place in Afro-American
literature. The preacher deserves admiration from
anyone who hears his poetry, either in his church
or by reading the renditions. They are not tran-
scriptions; they are not exercises in linguistic
reproduction. But they are authentic, dignified,
reverent, and they are, indeed, gems of American
Literature.

CHAPTER 4 . . . . .WALTER WHITE:
           "The Preacher's Mask"

> "I remember when I first started
> preaching over at Valdosta. I
> was just out of school and was
> filled up with ambition to raise
> my people out of their igno-
> rance. I was determined I would
> free them from a religion that
> didn't do anything for them but
> make them shout and holler on
> Sunday. I was going to give
> them some modern religion based
> on intelligence instead of just
> on feeling and emotion."
>
> --Walter White, The Fire in the
>   Flint

Walter F. White (1893-1955) was born in Atlanta
and spent his youth and early adult life there.
He was graduated from Atlanta University in 1916
and entered the insurance business. The Atlanta
race riot in the fall of 1906 left a lasting impression on the young White who joined the fledg-
ling NAACP in its fight to prevent the Atlanta
school board from curtailing the already limited
annual terms in black public schools in order to
provide more money for strengthening white
schools. In 1918, White joined the national office of the NAACP as assistant secretary and remained with that organization for the remainder
of his active public life. He was especially
active in the anti-lynching programs of the
Association, using field investigations, media
reporting, formal reports, and creative writing
as his arsenal for fighting that hated American
institution. In addition to magazine articles
in American Mercury, Century, and Nation, White
wrote a regular column for the Pittsburgh
Courier, one of the most prominent of several

black national weekly newspapers published during the first half of the 20th century. His major books include his two novels--The Fire in the Flint (1924) and Flight (1926); Rope and Faggot: Biography of Judge Lynch, A Study of Lynching (1929); his autobiography, A Man Called White (1948); and his last work on race relations, How Far the Promised Land (1955). The essay on White's image of the preacher is based on portions of his The Fire in the Flint.

"The Fire in the Flint"

Robert A. Bone, in his The Negro Novel in America, calls Walter White's The Fire in the Flint (1924) "an anti-lynching tract of melodramatic proportions," little more than a "series of essays, strung on an unconvincing plot, involving the misfortunes of a colored doctor and his family in a small Southern town." Bone writes as a literary historian who seldom understands the nuances of Afro-American writers' tone and purpose in their literature. White, best-known as long-time Field Secretary of the National Association for the Advancement of Colored People (NAACP) would hardly have considered himself a significant creative writer. His organization focused its word and attention on lynching as a national menace, particularly in the years between the close of World War I and the Depression. White knew the difference between an essay and a novel. His two novels, The Fire in the Flint and Flight appeared during the Harlem Renaissance, that period during which white Americans rediscovered the culture of black Americans. Black poets and fiction writers attracted national attention on an unprecedented scale. Paul Laurence Dunbar and Charles Chesnutt, in particular, had gained some recognition in a previous era. After World War I a combination of factors spawned a new importance for literature about the black American experience: white writers became interested in black people;

popular black music fostered a new type of black-
white interaction, particularly in Harlem; and
the post-war generation of Afro-Americans expressed a racial image that tended to make the nation
keenly aware of its race problems; and organiza-
tiona like the NAACP and the National Urban
League had among their leaders W.E.B DuBois and
James Weldon Johnson, literary artists as well as
civil rights leaders and Charles S. Johnson who
nurtured black writers and black writing in his
Opportunity Magazine. Black writers were in
vogue. Literature they produced became a significant medium, along with social advancement movements, for expressing the vitality of the "New
Negro" metaphor. This artistic and activist
force dominated literary and political activities
during the period. White established contact
and influence with many important national personalities. He fully understood the power literature exercised upon the nation. As Field
Secretary for NAACP, he was as qualified as any
American to describe and interpret race relations
in the nation. His personal and professional experiences uniquely qualified him to use his talents as a writer in a period in which black poets
and novelists found a new strength in literature
and art.

White wrote The Fire in the Flint in twelve
days. In it, he dramatized the heinous practice
of lynching and its kind of genocide of black
Americans. Moreover, the novel's plot hurls a
bitter denunciation at the "accommodationist"
social philosophy most often associated with
Booker T. Washington. Instead, it advocates the
position of the "New Negro" who longs for first-
class citizenship for black Americans even as
slaves dreamed of emancipation. The aspirations
are the same, but the approaches to them are different. In earlier times, black Americans asked
for and pled to be allowed to enjoy the promise
of American democracy and the fruits of their
labors for the country. Since World War I, they
had chided their nation for having gone to "make

the world safe for democracy" in Europe, as President Woodrow Wilson's declaration of war on the Central Powers had stated the national purpose, without improving the social and political status of black Americans at home.

Kenneth B. Harper, M.D., black, young doctor who chooses to practice medicine in his small hometown in Georgia, illustrates the crisis between the "accommodationist" and the "radical" among black Americans. He hopes for a reasonable part of the American dream, but he is agitated by the prevailing belief that "no Negro is fit to participate in government due to his limited education, his lack of experience, his criminal tendencies and more especially, to his helpless mental and pyhsical inferiority to the white race." He had been educated in medical schools and hospitals in the urban centers of the United States and in Europe, and he did not consider himself inferior to white citizens in his town, intellectually, socially, morally, nor physically. He rejected the philosophy his father had expressed to him in their last talk:

Any Negro can get along without trouble in the South if he only attends his own business. It was unfortunate, mighty unpleasant and uncomfortable at times, that colored people, no matter what their standing, had to ride the jimcrow cars, couldn't vote, couldn't use the public libraries and all those other things. Lynching, too, was bad. But only bad Negroes ever got lynched. And after all, those things weren't all of life. Booker Washington was right and the others who were always howling about rights were wrong. Get a trade or a profession. Get a home. Get some property. Get a bank account. Do something! Be somebody! And then, when enough Negroes had reached that stage, the ballot and all the other things now denied them would come. White folks then would see that the Negroes

72

was deserving of those rights and priv-
ileges and would freely, gladly give them
to him without his asking for them.

This was not "New Negro" talk. Yet, young
Dr. Harper seemed to believe his special status
as a physicain somehow separated him from the
fate his fellow black men and women faced in his
town. He does not believe in the "accommodationist" view of life but he realizes he is accommo-
dating his personal aspiration and self-image to
what the white society imposes upon him. The
novel presents a scathing attack on the social
values and behavior of Southern American society.
The specific focus is upon the humiliation well-
educated professional black persons feel when
their talents and industry have not brought them
genuine respect from their communities.

Fire in the Flint provides an image of the
preacher within this context. Reverend Ezekiel
Wilson, pastor of Mt. Zion Baptist Church in Harper's hometown, becomes a soul mate with the physician. Their roles exemplify the tension their
kind faces in a world that does not reward dili-
gence and morally correctness as Booker T. Washington had promised. Withdrawal is one option
as a scheme of survival in such an environment,
as persons in this stance sometimes don the mask
that diminishes them in return for personal safety. White believes this compromise is a personal tragedy, and that it should be avoided at
any cost. Activism is a worthy alternative.

Inevitably, Wilson and Harper would cross
paths. The doctor would be expected to associate himself with the church in the town in which
he practiced medicine. And it was his hometown.
A few weeks after he had established his office
as a part of the family home, Harper attended
the Mt. Zion Baptist Church in company with his
mother, sister, and younger brother. He did not
go merely as a duty. The visible essence of the
socio-economic intransigence in the town showed

itself in the church. Harper noticed it had
changed little. It was a little more dilapidated
than he remembered it. The same groups of people
stood before the door, eagerly snatching words
of conversation before entering. Young men,
"garbed in raiment of varied and brilliant hue,
ogling the girls as they passed in with their
parents" reminded Harper of the days of his own
youth. He recalled arguing with a boy who attended the Methodist Church nearby about whether
Mt. Zion Baptist Church was "the biggest and
finest church in the whole world." Now, he
smiled as he thought briefly of Notre Dame in
Paris and St. Paul's in London. He had seen them
during his medical studies and military service
in Europe. But, as if to emphasize so large and
stubborn a part of the theme of the novel, the
author indicates this church has changed very
little. It contained the same rows of hard seats
worn shiny by years of use, the same choir loft
to the left of the pulpit with its faded red cur-
tains, the same worn Bible upon the pulpit beside the a hymn book, the same ornately carved
silver pitcher and goblet. That particular Sunday morning, Harper felt as though he had never
left Central City when he looked for and found
patches of calcimine hanging from the ceiling
and the yellowed marks on the walls made by the
dripping from leaks in the roof. As the hum of
conversation ceased, the pastor entered the pulpit from a little door behind it. The choir
sang the doxoloxy and all the familiar services
came back to Kenneth as he sat and looked at the
dusky faces around him. When the preliminaries
had ended, the Reverend Wilson began to preach.
He was a fat, pompous, oily man with a smooth
and unctuous manner. His voice sank at times to
a whisper--at others, roared until the rafters
of the building seemed to ring with its echo.
He played on it as consciously as the dried-up
little organist in the gaily colored bonnet did
on the keys of the asthmatic little organ. That
morning his text was taken from the 13th Chapter
of I Corinthians 1st verse--"Though I speak

74

with tongues of men and of angels, and have not charity, I am become as sounding brass, or a tinkling cymbal."

Slowly and softly, the Reverend Wilson began to preach. His manner was conventional and appropriate:

Breddern and sisters, they's a lot of you folks right here this mawnin' what thinks you is Christ'uns. You think jus' 'cause you comes here ev'ry Sunday and sings and shouts and rants around dat you is got the sperit of Jesus in you. Well, I'm tellin' you this mawnin' dat you'd better wake up and get yo'self right with God, 'cause you ain't no mo Christ'un dan if you nevah been to chu'ch a-tall. De Good Book says you got to have char'ty, and de Good Book don't lie.

To the accompaniment of "Amen!" "Ain't it the truth!" and other approbations from his congregation, the minister lashed out at the sins of his flock. He painted a vivid and uncomfortably realistic picture of a burning Hell into which all sinners would inevitably be cast. Almost with the air of a hypnotist he gradually advanced the tempo of his speech. Like a wind playing over a field of corn, swaying the tops of the stalks at will, so did he play on the emotions and fears and passions of his congregation. Only a master of human psychology could have done that, the author explains. It was a living, breathing vengeful God he preached and his auditors fearfully swayed and rocked to and fro as he lashed them unmercifully. Frequently, the preacher would, without perceptible pause, swing into a rolling, swinging, half-moaning song which the congregation took up with fervor. The beat was steadily advanced by the leader until he and his audience were worked up to an emotional ecstasy bordering on hysteria. When this part of his performance was ended, the preacher

75

painted a glowing picture of the ineffable peace
and joy that would come to those who rested their
faith in Him who died for the remission of their
sins.

As Kenneth walked home that morning, he wondered whether that kind of religious fervor was
good for his people. He knew he hoped the church
would attract some intelligent and able young men
who, unlike what he saw in Reverend Wilson, could
become a 20th century Moses and lead his people
out of the thraldom of this primitive religion.
But he also wondered whether such a Moses could
offer a solace that would offer black people a
way to bear their burdens such as that which men
like Wilson could provide. As these questions
raced across his mind, a new awareness of the
complexities of the race problem took hold of
Harper. He saw his people kept in bondage of ignorance and asked why. At this moment, the answer was simple: it was to the advantage of the
white South to have it so. But why was a man
like Wilson patted on the back and every old
Negro who resented the brutalities and proscrip-
tions of race prejudice instantly labeled a
radical--a dangerous character--one seeking "social equality"? Pondering these matters made
Harper feel like a squirrel traveling around in
a circular cage. No matter where he started or
how far he revealed, he always wound up at the
same point and with the same sense of blind de-
feat. So, once more, he decided for the moment
it was better for him to stay to himself, attend
to his own business, and let these problems go.
In spite of himself, though, he often found himself enmeshed in this endless quandary. Just as
frequently, he determined to put from himself
again the insoluble problem.

The brutal murder of Bud Ware, a black man
in the town, was the specific act which brought
Kenneth Harper and the Reverend Wilson together.
The growing uneasiness which the doctor experi-
enced--uneasiness and discomfort about the pa-

thetic helplessness of black men and women in his own town--caused him to cast about for someone to talk with about the matter. Reverend Wilson?, he asked himself. He was ignorant and coarse, but he had lived in South Georgia all his life and he would know better what to do than anybody else. So he determined to go to talk with the minister that evening as soon as he was free. He had hardly made the decision when the Reverend Wilson himself entered the young doctor's reception room and called out to Kenneth as he sat in his office:

> Good Mawnin', Brudder Harper. It certainly has done my heart good to see you attendin' chu'ch ev'ry Sunday with your folks. Mos' of these young men and women, as soon's they get some learning, thinks they's too good to 'tend chu'ch. But, as I says to them all th' time, th' Lawd ain't goin' t' bless none of them, even if they is educated, if they don't keep close to him.

As Kenneth rose to move toward his visitor with inward repugnance; the coarseness of the man repelled him. Wilson seemed overheated even in the coldest weather, and his face shone with a greasiness that seemed to indicate his body excreted oil instead of perspiration. Yet, this man could give him some ray of hope, if there was any to be had. So he told Wilson of his experiences of the past two days. He had attempted to register the murder of Bud Ware as was required by law, but the brother of the man who had killed him--who also happened to be the County Clerk-- refused to issue a certificate of registration of the death. The preacher's eyes widened with a mild surprise and what seemed to the young doctor a benevolent mask which he wore most of the time. He listened through Kenneth's comments without any response. Suddenly, though, he dropped his illiterate speech much to Kenneth's surprise when he finally spoke:

> Dr. Harper, I've been watching you since

you came back here. I knew that you were
trying to keep away from this trouble
that's always going on around here. That's
just why I came here to-day. Your case is
a hard one, but it's small to what a lot
of these others are feeling. I have asked
a number of the more sensible coloured men
to meet at my house to-night. I think it
would be a good thing to talk over these
things and try to find a way to avoid any
trouble.

Naturally, young Harper looked up with surprise, not at the idea of holding a meeting, but
at the sudden change in the language the man was
using. When he openly commented upon the difference in speech the minister laughed:

There's a reason--in fact, there are two
reasons why I talk like that. The first
is because of my own folks. Outside of
you and your folks, the Phillips family,
and one or two more, all of my congregation is made up of folks with little or
no education. They've all got good hard
common sense, it's true. They'd have to
have that in order just to live in the
South with things as they are. But they
don't want a preacher that's too far above
them--they'll feel that they can't come
to him and tell him their troubles if
he's too highfalutin. I try to get right
down to my folks, feel as they feel, suffer when they suffer, laugh with them when
they laugh, and talk with them in language
they can understand.

And the minister smiled, almost to himself,
as memories of contacts with his lowly flock came
to him, and continued:

I remember when I first started preaching
over at Valdosta. I was just out of school
and was filled up with the ambition to raise

78

my people out of their ignorance. I was
determined I would free them from a religion that didn't do anything for them but
make them shout and holler on Sunday. I
was going to give them some modern religion
based on intelligence instead of just on
feeling and emotion. . . . I preached to
them and told them of Aristotle and Shakespeare and Socrates. One Sunday, after I'd
preached what I thought was a mighty fine
sermon, one old woman came up after the
services and said to me: 'Brer Wilson, dat's
a' right tellin' us 'bout Shakespeare and
Homer and all dem other boys. But what we
want is for you t' tell us somethin' 'bout
Jesus!'

Kenneth Harper laughed with the preacher at
the old woman's insistence on not straying from
the religion she had been used to and the preacher explained that he had to discard his high-
flown theories and come down to his folks if he
wanted to do any good at all:

These same folks, however, don't want you
to come down too close. Like all people
with little education, whether they're
black, white, or any other colour, they
like to look up to their leaders. So I
use a few big words now and then which
have a grand and rolling sound, and they
feel that I am even more wonderful because
I do know how to use big words but don't
use them often.

Kenneth saw the preacher in a new light. He
had known the Mr. Wilson, many years before coming to Central City, had attended a theological
seminary in Atlanta and had wondered how a man
could attend a school of theology of any standing
and yet use such poor English. It had never occurred to him that it might be deliberate. "And
then there's another, reason," continued Reverend
Wilson. "The white folks here are mighty suspi-

79

cious of any Negro who has too much learning,
according to their standards." He explained
that whites would figure that any educated Negro
would stir up other blacks to fight back when
trouble arose. He had decided many years ago
that someone had to help the poor black people
in the community bear their burdens and comfort
them. He knew if he came out and said the things
he thought and felt he would either be taken out
of his home some night and lynched or he would
be run out of town. He decided that he would
smile and bear it and be what the white folks
thought they wanted him to be. That role had
been difficult at times but he said that the Lord
had given him the strength somehow or other to
stand it so far. And with his deliberately im-
perfect English, there had gone from the preacher's face the subservient smile. Kenneth felt
his heart warming to the man, his distaste and
repulsion dissipating, now that the shell had
been removed and he saw beneath the surface.
Most of all, he learned a new social truth: that
the Negro in the South had many things in common
with the chameleon--that he had to be able to
change his colour figuratively to suit his environment in order to stay alive.

Dr. Kenneth Harper, together with Reverend
Ezekiel Wilson, the Reverend Richard Young of the
Bethel AME Church, Herbert Phillips, Tom Tracy,
Hiram Tucker, and James Swan organized a share-
croppers' organization to help alleviate the
destitute condition of the black farmers in the
county whose eternal indebtedness to the men who
owned the land they farmed enslaved them. Their
organization prospered and created a serious
threat to the landowners, the merchants and the
bankers of Central City. Finally, this venture,
brought about largely through the new mutual respect and cooperative effort of Harper and
Wilson, led to the young doctor's own death.
When he was called to treat the daughter of a
leading white merchant in town, the Ku Klux Klan
claimed he had gone to the white merchant's

house to criminally assault the man's wife and
daughter.

The community--his own hometown--to which
the Young Dr. Kenneth Harper had returned to work
among his people became the grounds upon which
he lost his life as a lynch victim.

For purposes of this discussion, though, a
unique image of the preacher stands out in bold
relief. For it is most unusual that any man
would be required by social circumstances and
through no fault of his own to denigrate himself
to the extent that he makes himself subject to
ridicule in order to be able to serve the purposes of his calling. Indeed, a society in which
the circumstance is found may very well qualify
to be called what James Baldwin terms the "plague
of Christianity." Kenneth Harper, physician, cannot gain even common respect as a man in the society in which he lives. Not even when he willingly saves the life of a beloved member of the
group who seeks to destroy him. Ezekiel Wilson,
Christian minister, avoids the explicit indigni-
ties which the young physician suffers. He does
not lose his life in the novel; he serves his
congregation effectively and well; he serves them
in the manner which they expect of him. But in
a larger sense, he is required to sell himself
short in order to perform his services at all.
In his union with Kenneth Larson and the few
other Negro leaders in the community, though, he
foreshadows the kind of minister so well-known
in the latter half of the 20th century who together with his church congregation provided a
basis for the social consciousness and social
action which vividly permeates the plot of
Walter White's The Fire in the Flint.

81

CHAPTER 5 . . . . ZORA NEALE HURSTON'S JOHN
                  PEARSON: Saint and Sinner

> John never made a balk at a
> prayer. Some new figure,
> some new praise-giving name
> for God, every time he knelt
> in church. He rolled his
> African drum up to the altar,
> and called his Congo Gods by
> Christian names. One night
> at the altar call he cried
> out his barbaric poetry to
> his "wonder-workin'" God: so
> effectively that three con-
> verts came thru religion un-
> der the sound of his voice.
>
> Zora Neale Hurston, Jonah's
> Gourdvine

Zora Neale Hurston (1907-1960) came to Washington, D.C., during her youth to study at Howard
University. She began writing there and became
an integral part of the Harlem Renaissance,
studying anthropology with Franz Boaz and earning
a bachelors degree at Barnard College in 1928.
She continued her interest in cultural studies
on Rosenwald and Guggenheim study and research
grants that took her to the West Indies and Haiti
to collect folklore. She contributed short stories and plays to a variety of "little" magazines, including Opportunity, Fire, and Story;
and published articles and stories in Saturday
Evening Post, New Republic, and American Mercury.
Hurston's major works include: Jonah's Gourdvine
(1934) a novel; Mules and Men (1935) a book of
folklore; Their Eyes Were watching God (1937) a
novel, and Dust Tracks on a Road (1943) her autobiography. The discussion of her image of a
preacher in this work centers around Jonah's
Gourdvine.

Zora Neale Hurston's qualifications to write about a black preacher and his life in his professional role is secured by that portion of her autobiography that reads:

> I tumbled right into the Missionary Baptist Church when I was born. I saw the preachers and the pulpits, the people and the pews. Both at home and from the pulpit, I heard my father, known to thousands as "Reverend Jon" (an abbreviation for John) explain about God's habits, His Heaven, His ways and means. Everything was known and settled. From the pews I heard a ready acceptance of all that Papa said. Feet beneath the pews beat out a rhythm as he pictured the scenery of heaven. Heads nodded with conviction in time to Papa's words. Tense snatches of tune broke out and some shouted until they fell into a trance at the recognition of what they heard from the pulpit. Come "love feast" some of the congregation told of getting close enough to peep into God's sittingroom windows. Some went further. They spoke of sights and scenes around God's throne.

Her Jonah's Gourdvine appeared toward the end of the Harlem Renaissance period in American letters. Unlike many works of the era, this novel is laid on the deep South. Critics have complained that Hurston ignored unpleasant social aspects of Southern life for blacks. One who reads Jonah carefully knows, however, that John Pearson, its central character, is always conscious of the nuances of racial tension, and his own statements about race pride show he believes he suffers when white people know too much about his family, community, and religious life. He is mulatto. But he is no "tragic" mulatto, cringing for his heritage that a white father withholds from him, nor one who considers himself superior to his fellowmen because of his

84

white blood. He suffers no identity problem in that respect. <u>Jonah</u> is not a protest novel and its picture of the South is incomplete. Hurston addresses, though, a refreshingly different vision of Afro-American life from most of her contemporaries among black writers. And her choice is fortuitous, for the novel combines her skill as social scientist and storyteller with her deeply personal experiences to produce an unusual insight and appreciation for the comprehensiveness and subtlety of the black American's unique religious life in the rural South. She uses social and cultural history that she expresses in authentic language and metaphor of the essential people who are the root and branch of the black American caught in the act of living.

John Pearson becomes a preacher early in the novel's plot. He is a memory for Hurston, but he is also a paradigm for the changing black community leader who tries desperately to respond to his setting as time passes. He is finally incapable of coping with those changes, but he has little control over them, either. He highlights without seeming to know he does, the change from a highly personal, oral society into a mechanical nation that agonizes over that seachange that swept through the race's psyche in the World War I period and the years that immediately followed. Hurston fashioned her preacher, as the touchstone of the upheaval, carefully, as a portion of a letter she wrote to James Weldon Johnson indicates:

> I have tried to present a Negro preacher who is neither funny nor an imitation Puritan ram-rod in pants. Just the human being and poet that he must be to succeed in a Negro pulpit. I do not speak of those among us who have been tampered with and consequently have gone Presbyterian or Episcopalian. I mean the common run of us who love magnificence, beauty, poet-

ry and color so much that there can never
be too much of it. Who do not feel that
the ridiculous has been achieved when
someone decorates a decoration. . . . I
see a preacher as a man outside of his
pulpit and so far as I am concerned he
should be free to follow his bent as other
men. He becomes the voice of the spirit,
when he ascends the rostrum.

Anyone familiar with the dynamics of the
black church and its relationship to its preacher knows the validity of the character of John
Pearson. Larry Neal's Introduction to the 1971
edition of Jonah illuminates the novel's meaning
when he explains that like all saints, Pearson
is constantly being tempted by the enticements
of the flesh; that his Christian will toward
agape is constantly under challenge by the carnal impulse. Such a tension requires in a
character two distinctly different attitudes
toward spirituality. One springs from a former-
ly enslaved communal society, non-Christian in
background where there is really no clean-cut
dichotomy between the world of flesh and the
spirit, and the other represents a rigid and
prescribed Puritan contempt for a part of the
tradition of white evangelism. The image is,
indeed, complex. But its logic and validity and
charm shine through the complexity. For, Hurston's preacher and his people were forced to
seem to accept a Christianity without making
provisions for their own established and authentic sense of religiosity which they brought in
their collected memory to the New World. These
aspects of his "pre-Christian cultural memory"
give rise to the unique forms of expression
found in the preaching of the Afro-American Man
of God. In the highest tradition of the mys-
teries of the universe upon which he has based
his unique ethos. The congregation knows him as
poet, prophet, and seer who speaks truths to his
people. The racial memory among his congregation will permit the preacher only a limited

86

amount of deviation from the common lore. He
may be heretical when he deviates from the American black religion and he may be impeached if
he abuses his administrative privilege beyond
the congregation's limits of reason. But he has
said he has been called of God, and if his people decide he has told the truth in that claim,
his prerogatives are broad.

The cosmography of Afro-American religion
appears from the very first line of Jonah. "God
was grumbling His thunder and playing the zigzag lightning thru his fingers," as Amy Crittendon, John Pearson's mother, looks to the clouds
and says to her husband, "Ole Massa gwinter
scrub floors today," indicating the poetry people like her use to ascribe to a God the power
of the universe, and illustrating the poetic
language they use in expressing their percep-
tions of that God. With these few sentences,
then, the author has authenticated the folklore
out of which the central character of the novel
emerges. No one in that world needs to be
trained to understand the religion of his eth-
nicity. It is a part of his daily life, at
least so far as the language of the religion is
concerned. The first half of the novel establishes the Son of Man image of the dichotomy of
Son of Man and Son of God.

John Pearson is Amy's "big son", whose
father was not Amy's present husband. Because
he had "uh li'l white folks color" in his face,
his stepfather predicted a calamity for him.
His "brazen ways wid dese white folks" was going
to get him lynched one of these days, the old
man argued; his mother tried to defend him, re-
minding her husband that he works harder than
anybody else on the place. Ned Crittendon makes
no secret of his dislike for John who, to him,
is a reminder of the light-complexioned slaves
the masters favored while black slaves, like
himself, were "s'posed tuh ketch de wind and de

weather." Amy, though, did not want any of her
children to come up like she and Ned had grown
up during slavery. She was 12 years old
when Lee surrendered, and although she did not
work particularly hard, she realized that her
children were different from both their parents.
Black folks could not love their children in
slavery because they actually belonged to their
masters. There was no need to treasure other
people's property, but now that "de big bell
done rung," black parents could love their own
children, and Amy intended to see that hers experienced love. John is clearly an emerging man
of the soil; he is 16 years old who could pass
for 20. In fact, Ned has agreed to "bind him
over" to Captain Mimms, an arrangement which
both Amy and John dislike. This family dis-
agreement leads Ned to take the whip to his wife,
bringing all his children to her defense, including John who proves he is a man by soundly
trouncing his step-father. Ned orders John off
the place.

So John put on his brass-toed shoes and his
clean shirt, ready to leave home. Amy dug out a
crumpled and mouldy dollar and gave it to him.
"Where you goin', son?" she asked, and John replied, "Over de Big Creek, mama. Ah ever wanted
tuh cross over." Amy walks "a piece of the way"
with him to the creek and confides to him that
he was born over the creek. In their parting,
John says he wants to make money so he can return and bring his mother to live with him. Amy
tells John about the dangers of the foot-log over
the Creek and the snakes near it, but her son
admits to her, "Ah done swum dat ole creek,
mama--'thout yuh knowin'," and he goes on his
way, exuding the Earth Man qualities which have
been ascribed to him to this point in the novel:

John plunged on down the Creek, singing a
new song and stomping the beats. The Big
Creek thundered among its rocks and wheeled
on down. So John sat on the foot-log and

made some words to go with the drums of
the Creek. Things walked in the birch
woods, creep, creep creep. The hound
dog's lyric crescendo lifted over and
above the tree tops. He was on the
foot-log, half way across the Big Creek
where maybe people laughed and maybe
people had lots of daughters. The moon
came up. The hunted coon panted down the
Creek, swam across and proceeded leisurely
up the other side. The tenor-singing
hound dog went home. Night passed. No
more Ned. No hurry. No telling how many
girls might be living on the new and shiny
side of the Big Creek. John almost trum-
peted exultantly at the new sun. He
breathed lustily. He stripped and crossed
his clothes across, then recrossed and
and plunged into the swift water and
breasted strongly over.

Elemental John has crossed the Creek--lit-
erally and symbolically--and immediately finds
thirty or forty children emerging from a log
building--the schoolhouse he has heard about--
and he realizes the wisdom of his choice to
leave home: "Negro children going to learn to
read and write like white folks. See! All this
going on over there and the younguns over the
Creek choppin' cotton!" As he stopped, leaned
over the fence and stared, one little girl stood
before him, arms akimbo and exclaimed, "Well,
Folks! Where you reckon dis big yaller, bee-
stung nigger come from?" When the others
laughed, John felt ashamed of his bare feet for
the first time in his life. The same little
girl asked why he, John, did not go to school
and directed him to find Alf Pearson whom his
mother had advised him to find in order to seek
a job. The same day, John saw a railroad train
for the first time in his life.

When he finds Alf Pearson, once more the
"elemental man" aspects of his character come

forth. "What a fine stud! Why, boy, you would have brought five thousand dollars on the block in slavery time," Alf Pearson exclaims when he sees John for the first time. Subtly, the author gives the hint that John is Pearson's son, sired while Amy, his mother, was a slave on that plantation. John was welcomed at the Pearson place, allowed to enter school, given a job which demanded little time, and provided clothes which his employer's son had discarded. At school, John quickly learns that the girls in the community will vie for his attention, and he is given, by the teacher, the surname "Pearson," inasmuch as he has none of his own. "Mama, she name me Two-Eye John," he tells the teacher. His mother had named him "from a preachin' man she heard," John explains, foreshadowing his later entry into the ministry and the character through which the author makes her most significant racial statement. John Pearson, on the first day he went to school, receives a complete name for the first time in his life, thereby receiving an identity which is authentic, especially if one accepts Alf Pearson as his father. Importantly, too, he has almost immediately singled out the one girl, among the many who court his favors, who interests him most--Lucy Ann Potts. She is the smallest and youngest of the girls in his circle. She becomes his wife later.

Most interesting, during the early days "over the Creek," John discovers a tiny clearing in the woods, which he recognizes as "a prayin' ground," and he immediately falls to his knees and prays:

> O Lawd, heah 'tis once mo' and again yo' weak and humble servant is knee-bent and body-bowed--Mah heart beneath mah knees and mah knees in some lonesome valley (*Note the almost verbatim relationship to James Weldon Johnson's "Prayer" from his God's Trombones.) cryin' fuh mercy

          whilst mercy kinst be found. O Lawd!
          you know my heart, and all de ranges uh
          mah deceitful mind--and if you find any
          sin lurkin' in and about mah heart please
          pluck it out and cast it tuh condemn me
          in de judgement.

     Here, for the first time in the novel, the
issues of the tension which emerge from the
Agape-Eros dichotomy are joined. John knows the
world of human sexuality; he has become a favorite hide-and-seek partner in the village; girls
have already argued over him. He needed no
training to understand his manhood in a carnal
sense; he also needed no instruction·to render
the prayer quoted above. Each has arisen from
the collected consciousness of which he was the
archetype, although he is the offspring of the
two racial strains of the nation--his mother is
a Negro ex-slave and his father is a white ex-
slave owner. In his own conscious actions, John
Pearson has juxtaposed the jarring elements of
his emerging characterization, as he does
throughout the novel. Immediately after the
morning that he utters the spontaneous prayer,
"that night, deaf to Mehaley's blandishments,
John sat in the doorway and told tales. And
Brer Rabbit and Brer Fox and Raw-Head and Bloody-
Bones walked the earth like natural men."

     A third and less pronounced issue of John's
development enters with his experiences in
school. They may be considered "Appolonian," in
a sense, but his education is elementary and
quickly reported in the narrative. Some of it
comes vicariously, in a sense; for Lucy Potts,
who to him is "almost uh fever now," is the one
member of the class no one can spell down. Her
spelling skill is almost apocryphal. He tells
his friend Charlie some say Lucy can spell "Con-
stantinople"! Her brother leads the choir at
the Macedonia Baptist Church and she trebles
alongside grown women, singing square, round,
and triangle notes.

Lucy becomes John's ambition. He sees her
every day at school and on Sunday at church.
She is always in his consciousness, but up to
this point, he has not talked to her alone.
Handling the other girls--Big "Oman, Lacey,
Semmis, Bootsie, and Mehaley--called for action;
but with Lucy he needed words he did not possess.
When he tells Lucy he wants to speak as she
speaks, she praises his good voice and encour-
ages him, but she also exercises a degree of
reservation with him which makes it clear she
requires special handling. And he is willing
and capable of showing toward Lucy all of the
skills he possesses. As Earth Man, he comple-
ments her early in their acquaintanceship when
he is alone with her for the first time. He has
heard she is the fastest runner in the school
and challenges her to a footrace which he wins
handily. Also he kills the snake which everyone
fears near the foot-log over the branch that separates the Pearson place from Lucy's family's
home. "Ooh, John, Ah'm sho glad you kilt dat
ole devil. He been right dere skeering folks
since befo' Ah wuz borned," Lucy cries. His
protective role establishes John as Lucy's lover
as he ceremoniously carries her three times back
and forth across the stream.

After a brief return to his home side of
the Creek to work with his step-father again,
John returns to Alf Pearson's plantation and becomes even more closely identified with his employer and in a semi-father and son relationship.
Now that he can read and write fairly well, he
takes charge of the commissary accounts, inasmuch as Alf Pearson's acknowledged son is still
studying in Paris. But his new position only
adds to the tension with the women. Mehaley
still badgers him about Lucy. He accedes to the
older girl's advances, but the next day he writes
Lucy's name in huge letters on the chimney of a
cabin nearby. Sunday, following, he was at
church "far ahead of enybody else," and he felt
good singing out of his three-cornered note hymn-

book until he saw Mehaley coming toward the
church. Once more the opposing elements of his
person become juxtaposed, as he falls down on
his knees and prays for cleansing. "He prayed
aloud and the empty house threw back his reso-
nant tones like a guitar box," and he enjoyed
the sound of his voice, so much so that he vowed
to pray in public soon as he retreated to the
safety of the choir-stand and out of Mehaley's
reach.

John resisted Mehaley and married Lucy Ann
Potts amid the stern disapproval of her family,
but with an advancement in his employment at the
plantation. The couple moved into house-ser-
vants' quarters and John's pay was raised. Significantly, Alf Pearson gave them, among other
wedding presents, a walnut bed with twisted
posts which Lucy treasured above all her posses-
sions. Mehaley continued with pursuit, even on
the morning following the birth of Lucy's first
baby. Within the next two or three years, John
had developed his own bevy of women, so much
that Alf Pearson warned him about meeting Big
'Oman in the commissary at night. "Dey done
tole you 'bout Big 'Oman and me?" John asked
Lucy one day, indicating a kind of honesty about
his infidelities that he practiced to the end of
his life, and Lucy admitted that she knew a
great deal about his activities. She suggested
he should go where his love lies and John replied, "Lucy, don't tell me nothin' 'bout leaving you, 'cause if you do dat, you'll make two
winters come in one year." And after a long
silence, he exhibited unusual self-understanding
in the following dialogue which, to a large extent, characterizes the novel's image of the
preacher:

> "Lucy, Ah love you and you alone. Ah
> swear Ah do. If Ah don't love you, God's
> gone tuh Dothan."

"What make you fool wid scrubs lak Big
'Oman and de rest of 'em?"

"Dat's the brute-beast in me. Ah sho
aim tuh live clean from dis on if you
'low me one mo' chance. Don't tongue-
lash me--jes' try me and see. Here you
done had three younguns fuh me and fixin'
to have un 'nother. Try me, Lucy."

Once more, the novel dramatizes almost painfully the ravaging dichotomy which plagues John
Pearson. His words above are spoken in earnestness, and they are further sanctioned by the action which follows:

The next big meeting John prayed in church,
and when he came to the final:

You are de same God, Ah
Data heard de sinner man cry.
Same God day sent de zigzag lightning tuh
Join de mutterin' thunder.
Same God dat holds de elements
In uh unbroken chain of controllment.
Same God dat hung on Cavalry and died,
Dat we might have a right tuh de tree of
    life--
We thank Thee that our sleeping couch
Was not our cooling board,
Our cover was not our winding sheet. . .
Please tuh give us uh resting place
Where we can praise Thy name forever,

                    Amen.

one deacon observed that "uh prayer went up tuhday," and another commented that John had plenty
fire in him and he had a "good, straining voice,"
and promised the deacons would call on him to
pray often.

The pre-Christian aspect of his personality
and of his religiosity--indeed, of the authen-

ticity of the dominant Afro-American religion--appears in the story of John Pearson in these words of the author of Jonah:

> John never made a balk at prayer. Some new figure, some new praise-giving name for God, every time he knelt in church. He rolled his African drum up to the altar, and called his Congo Gods by Christian names. One night at the altar call he cried out his barbaric poetry to his "wonder-workin' God" so effectively that three converts came thru religion under the sound of his voice.

He was called to preach, members of the church observed with sincerity, Deacon Moss was going to tell John that he had been called to preach, but he never had the chance to do so because John was at home and at church seldom. Lucy's time for the birth of a new baby was drawing nigh, but a woman named Delphine had drifted into town from Opelika and John had been away from home and the church almost continually for the next month. When he did return, once more he showed that side of his Earth Man quality which caused him to seek strenuously to show himself the provider for his family. Lucy's brother had come to demand payment of money John owed him. Finding him away and Lucy unable to pay the money, Bud had taken the bed which Alf Pearson had given to the young couple in payment of his loan. When John returned and found his new baby and his wife sleeping on a mattress on the floor, he searched out Bud, beat him severely, stole a hog which he used to bring meat home for his family, and ended up leaving town just ahead of the sheriff's posse.

Moving this time into central Florida which serves as the location for most of the significant action of the novel, John Pearson shifted, as had become his habit now, between free-wheeling sexual activity and the church. Working in

a railroad workers' camp, John went into town
one Sunday and heard a preacher whose delivery
intrigued him. Back at camp that night, he
preached the sermon he had heard that morning
for the entertainment of the crowd that listened
half in awe and half in laughter. "You can mark
folks," said Blue. "Dass jes' lak dat preacher
fuh de world. Pity you ain't preaching yo'self."
"Look, John," another fellow-worker told him,
"dey's un colored town out cross de woods uh
piece--maybe fifteen tuh twenty miles, and dey's
uh preacher . . . ." Before he could finish his
statement, John broke in to ask, "You mean uh
whole town uh nothin' but colored folks. Who
bosses it, den?" He was told the people in the
town themselves with their own mayor and corpo-
ration. He also learned there was a Methodist
preacher in the town who talked through his
nose.

When John went to visit Eatonville the next
week, he was most favorably impressed with the
Negro town. As he left that Sunday night, he
told a friend he would return; that he wanted to
bring his wife and children to live in that town.
He had intended to return with his family next
payday, but a new collection of women visitors
to the work camp delayed those plans for longer
than he wished. But with the return of his
strong resolve, he wrote Alf Pearson and sent
the money for the passage of his family to
Eatonville. When Lucy arrived, he showed her
once more his deep affection by not permitting
her to walk down the steps of the train. He
held his arms wide and made her jump into his
bosom, enjoying hearing her and the children ex-
claim at the fruit which was clustered on the
trees on the road to town. Lucy's sagacity,
which he had always respected, assumed the leadership for the entire family for a few months,
as she encouraged John to practice his skill in
carpentry, to buy a plot of ground, and to eventually build his own house. As they moved into
their new home, John's pride abounded as he

asked Lucy if she was sorry she had married him
instead of some fellow with a "whole heap of
money and titles hung on to him"; and in the
course of their conversation on this matter,
Lucy again mentioned his incontinuence to which
he explained: "Don't tell me 'bout dem trashy
women Ah lusts after once in uh while. Dey's
less dan leaves uh grass. Lucy do you still love
me lak yuh useter?" Yes, and more, she assured
him, confessing that she loved him then more
than ever. In his happiness he promised her he
could "take a job cleaning out de Atlantic Ocean"
just for her. He just couldn't get used to the
thought that she had married him and had had
children by him, he said.

Again, the juxtaposition of saint and sinner comes into the narrative as John rises in
Covenant Meeting next Sunday and starts the song,
"He's a Battle-Axe in de time Uh Trouble," and
when it was done he said, "Brothers and Sisters,
Ah rise befo' yuh tuhday tuh tell yuh, God done
called me tuh preach." And he continued, "He
called me long uhgo but Ah wouldn't heed tuh de
voice, but brothers and sisters, God done
whipped me tuh it, and liker Peter and Paul Ah
means to preach Christ and Him crucified. He
told me tuh go, and He'd go with me, so Ah ast
yo' prayers, Church, dat Ah may hold up de blood-
stained banner of Christ and prove strong dat Ah
may hold out to de end."

In this manner, John Pearson became a
preacher. The church agreed with his decision,
and predicted that he would be a battle-axe who
would win sinners to repentance. So many people
wanted to hear his trial sermon that it had to
be preached in a larger church. He had been
called to a pastorate before the hands had been
laid on his head, and people said that the man
who preached his ordination sermon was thrown in
a deep shadow by the preaching of the man who
was ordained. The church he pastored at Oconee
did all it could to hold him, but its membership

was less than 100. Zion Hope, the big church in
Sanford with a membership of more than 300,
called him as pastor. Thus, John Pearson had
become a black preacher in the United States,
and he represented one of the most complex
images of the ministry which is to be found in
Christianity. He has already been a Son of Man,
but he has been compelled toward preaching, moving him to become the Son of God, as one who
chose the vocation willingly and one whose choice
was sanctioned fervently by those who knew him.

Handling the tensions which lie inherently
in these polar and simultaneous roles which meet
in one man becomes the essence of the second half
of the novel. John Pearson's character as a man
has been set clearly. He loves women and they
love him. He also loves his wife, Lucy, and he
has often repeated his vows of devotion to her
and to her welfare. He has remained grateful to
her for marrying him; he has not mentioned the
sacrifices she made in going against her family's
wishes in her marriage, but he has remained sensitive about that decision. He has clearly
stated his double standard for the behavior of
husband and wife--in his own family--even when
Lucy mentions in jest that if John is tired of
her he can just leave, for there is another man
"over the fence" waiting for his job. But Pearson does not joke about even the thought of
another man for Lucy. He tells her firmly:

> "Li'l Bit, Ah ain't never laid de weight
> uh mah hand on you in malice. Ain't
> never raised mah hand tuh yuh eben when
> you gets mad and slaps mah jaws, but lemme
> tell you somethin' right now, and it ain't
> two, don't you never tell me no mo' whut
> you just tole me, 'cause if you do, Ahm
> goin' tuh kill you jes' ez sho ez gun is
> iron. Ain't never no man tuh breathe in
> yo' face but me. You hear me? What mad
> you say dat nohow?"

When Lucy explains, wisely, that it is just a by-word all women say, John makes it clear that she is not to say it; for no matter what comes or goes, if she ever starts out of the door to leave him, she will never make it to the gate; he will blow her heart out and hang for it. This threat is real and to him it in no way conflicts with his being a preacher. His woman and his religion are two entirely different matters, and his extra-marital affairs, his marriage, and his religion are separate matters to him. They are not equal; for most times, he places his devotion to and appreciation for Lucy above his concern for the church. When he speaks to Lucy, the other women are of no importance to him whatsoever. But he continues to associate with them throughout his marriage to her.

Author Hurston writes that John Pearson wore the cloak of a cloud about his shoulders. He was above the earth. He preached and prayed. He sang and sinned, but men saw his cloak and felt it. That, to the author, is the role of the preacher in the black experience. When Pearson explained to Lucy his own feelings about the natural poetry he produced and how being such a poet felt, he said: "Lucy, look Ah jus' found out whut Ah kin do. De words dat sets de church on fire comes tuh me jus' so. Ah reckon de angels must tell 'em tuh me." Speaking the voice of wisdom as it is perceived by a preacher's wife and at the same time by a member of the ethnic group from which he comes and with which he works, Lucy tells him, "God don't call no man, John, and turn 'im loose uh fool. Jus' you handle yo' members right and youse goin' tuh be uh sho 'nuff big nigger." When John retorts that he is treating his members right, and asks Lucy whether she has heard any complaints, she warns him with the sobering words:

> Naw, you wouldn't hear no complaints
> 'cause you treatin' 'em too good. Don't
> pump up dem deacons so much. Dey'll
> swell up and be de ruination of yuh.

99

Much up de young folks and you got
somebody tuh strain wid dem ole rams
when dey git habits on. You lissen
tuh me. Ah hauled de mud to make ole
Cuffy. Ah know whuts in 'im. . . . Don't
syndicate wid none of 'em, do dey'll put
your business in the street. . . . Friend
wid few. Everybody grin in yo' face don't
love yuh. Anybody kin look and see and
tell uh snake trail when dey come cross it
but nobody hin tell which way he wuz goin'
lessen he seen the snake. You keep outa
sight, and in day way, you won't give
nobody uh stick tuh crack yo' head wid.

The sinner-saint complex revolves most often
around John Pearson as preacher and John Pearson
as lover, as we have seen, but one incident
which provides a bit of humor in the story also
seems perfectly valid. Pearson runs for mayor
of his town and wins the election, but his op-
ponent claimed mildly that the contest was unfair. "It was the way you and Lucy led de gran'
march night 'fo' las' at the hall," he complained.
By rights, a preacher "ain't got no business
dancin'." Grand marching isn't dancing, Pearson
explained, and he never cut a step in the grand
march. That's right, another member of the
community said, "you ain't dancin' 'till yuh
cross yo' feet, but Reverend John, no sinner man
couldn't uh led dat march no better'n you and
Lucy. Dat li'l 'oman steps it lightly, slightly
and politely."

John was called to churches throughout the
state to conduct revivals and he was spoken of
as "The Battle-Axe." Lucy loved his primitive
poetry and magnificent pulpit gestures more than
ever, but she knew there was another woman in
the picture. She was pregnant again and prayed
to quit "feedin' on heart meat" as she had been
doing, else the baby would be affected. "Lawd,
if Ah meet dat woman in heben, you got tuh gimme

100

time tuh fight uh while," she said in her prayer over the dish-pan one morning. This was her second baby since coming to Florida, and she hoped its coming would change things. It did, for as soon as the baby was old enough, John took it along with Lucy to his church in Sanford and proudly displayed it to his congregation. But she knew even that day that a coldness in her husband fell upon her like dew, even as he preached before inviting all the congregation to pass by and look at his new baby. The coldness sickened her, but Lucy knew that her husband's successes would make her brother and his stepfather recognize him for the glory he enjoyed. She manuevered so that John became Moderator of the State Baptist Association, and she reflected pride as he gloated on that date: "Wisht old Ned and Bud could see me now, always makin' out Ah wuzn't goin' tuh be nothin'." He swaggered in his dark blue broadcloth, his hand-made alligator shoes, and his black Stetson hats. He usually left Lucy sitting on the front porch and she cried often. When she knew who the woman was, she felt more troubled to realize that John did not care that she did know. Even the sickness of their youngest daughter did not bring John and Lucy together as they had been. Instead, Pearson, standing around the bed of the child who was suffering from typhoid exclaimed, "Ah can't stand 'round and see mah baby girl die. Lucy! Lucy! God don't love me. Ah got to go 'way 'til it's all over. Ah jus' can't stay." So Lucy stayed at the baby's bedside while John fled to Tampa, gutted with grief until Hattie Tyson joined him for a week. When he returned the child was recovering. He brought Lucy a new dress and a pineapple.

What a church requires of its preacher-- his role as a saint--came into focus soon. Lucy attempted to warn John, but he considered her warnings nagging. "You either got tuh stop lovin' Hattie Tyson uh you got tuh stop preaching," she told him the people were saying. John

101

could not bring himself to express his temporary
relief to Lucy, nor to acknowledge that her advice had worked well. He simply brought her a
dozen mangoes and thrust them into her hand. As
they prepared for bed, Lucy asked, "Whut tex'
you goin' to preach on Sunday comin'?" When
John answered that it was communion Sunday and
he would preach on the Passover Supper in the
upper room, Lucy suggested, instead, that he
should preach a sermon on himself and call to
his congregation's memory some of the good things
he had done at the church. "Mah chillun, Papa
Pearson don't feel lak preachin' y'all tuh day,"
he began on Sunday after he had sung a song, and
he continued:

> y'all been looking at me fuh eight years
> now, but look lak some uh y'all been
> lookin' on me wid unseein' eye. When
> Ah speak tuh yuh from dis pulpit, dat
> ain't me talkin', dat's de voice uh God
> speakin' thru me. When de voice is thew,
> Ah jus' uhnother one uh God's crumblin'
> clods. Dere's seben younguns at mah
> house and Ah could line 'em all up in de
> courthouse and swear tuh eve'yone of 'em,
> Ahm uh natchel man but look lak some uh
> y'all is dumb tuh de fack.
>
> Course, mah childun in Christ, Ah been
> here wid y'all fuh eight years and mo'.
> Ah done set by yo' bedside and buried
> de dead and joined tuhgether de hands
> uh de livin', but Ah ain't got no
> remembrance. Don't keer if Ah laugh,
> don't keer if Ah cry, when de sun, wid
> his blood red eye, go intuh his house
> at night, he takes all mah remembrance
> wid 'im, but some yuh y'all dat got
> remembrance wid sich long tangues,
> dat it kin talk tuh yuh at a distance,
> when y'all is settin' down and passin'
> nations thew yo' mouf, look close and

see if in all mah doin's if dere wuz
anything good mingled up uhmoungst de
harm Ah done yuh. Ah ain't got no mind.
Y'all is de one dat is so much-knowin'
dat you kin set in judgement.

Maybe y'all got yo' right hand uh feller-
ship hid behind yuh. De Lawd's supper is
heah befo' us on de table. Maybe mah
hands ain't tuh tetch de cup no mo'. So
Ahm comin' down from the pulpit and Ah
ain't never goin' back lessen Ah go wid
yo hearts keepin' comp'ny wid mine and
yo' fire piled on mah fire, heapin' up.

He closed the great Bible slowly, passed
his handkerchief across his face and turned from
the pulpit, but when he made to step down, strong
hands were there to thrust him back. The church
surged up, a weeping wave about him. Deacons
Hambo and Harris were the first to lay hands
upon him. His weight seemed nothin in many
hands while he was roughly, lovingly forced back
into his throne-like seat. After a few minutes
of concerted weeping, he moved down to the Communion table and in a feeling whisper went thru
the sacrifice of a God.

When Lucy fell ill and died, John felt free;
at least he thought he felt free. He wanted to
feel he no longer felt guilt; there was no more
sin. He was merely a free man having his will
with women. In a sense, he was glad in his sad-
ness. At least, he thought he was. Within
three months after Lucy's death, Deacons Hambo,
Watson, Hoffman, and Harris called on John Pearson in his study at the parsonage to ask him if
he had married Hattie Tyson. He said he had,
and when the officers of the church complained
that he had "done jumped up and married" before
his wife had "got col' in her grave," John explained that he had to have someone to see after
his children. His friends said the children
were not being taken care of; that they were

103

running around the streets "jes' ez raggedy ez jay-birds in whistlin' time"; that they knew Hattie well and believed, from her past behavior and her following the sawmill camps throughout the state, the parsonage nor the children would interest her. When John objected to the uncomplimentary references to his wife, they were only more critical, all of which Hattie heard from another room. John was a broken man and wept over his confrontation with the deacons, largely because one of them was his closest friend, but Hattie revealed to her husband the piece of John-de-Conquerer root she was wearing in her hair and declared that no one could harm her with the root's protection. Too, she upbraided John for allowing the officers to come into his house and talk "'bout yo' wife lak she wuz a dog." Hattie said she no longer wondered why Lucy was dead if she had to endure similar insults.

Perhaps the author's view of the preacher becomes most obvious when she expresses it in a more cosmic sense than the particular details of his relations with his church. She compresses time and action into one summary statement which links John Pearson and the events of his life to those of any leader, inside and outside the dimensions of Christianity or even the species of human kind:

> The Lord of the Wheel that turns on itself slept, but the world kept spinning, and the troubled years sped on. Tales of weakness, tales of vice hung about John Pearson's graying head. Tales of wifely incontinence which Zion Hill swallowed hard. The old ones especially. Sitting coolly in the shade of the after-life, they looked with utter lack of tolerance upon the brawls of Hattie and John. They heard her complaints often and believed her only refused action because they knew the complainant to be

equally as guilty, but less popular than
the man against whom she cried. Besides,
the younger generation winked at what
their elders cried over. Lucy had coun-
selled well, but there were those who
exhulted in John's ignominious fall from
the Moderatorship after nine years' tenure,
and milled about him like a wolf pack
about a tired old bull-looking for a throat-
hold, but he still had enough of his Pagan
poesy to thrill. The pack waited. John
knew it was tired unto death of fighting
off the struggle which must surely come.
The devouring forces of the future leered
at him at unexpected moments. Then too
his daily self seemed to be wearing thin,
and the past seeped thru and mastered him
for increasingly longer periods. He whose
present had always been so bubbling that
it crowded out past and future now found
himself with a memory.

And that memory was his pain. His marriage
to Hattie troubled him in comparison with his
guilty memory of Lucy. When Hattie asks him
whether he wants her to love him any more, he
replies, "Naw. . . . It don't seem lak iss clean
uh sumpin." She was like a blowfly to him, he
said; she spoiled everything she touched. She
certainly was no Lucy. Hattie agreed, arguing
that she was not going to "cloak" for him nor
to take off him what Lucy took. Moreover, she
threatened to "pull the cover off" John and his
newest lover, adding, "Ah ain't gonna be no ole
man's fool." Then, as in a trance, John recalls
vividly the picture of Lucy seven years ago, her
bright eyes in the sunken face, as she lay helpless and defenseless when he struck her shortly
before her death, motivated by his guilt. That
expression on Lucy's face caused John to stare
in fascinated horror for a moment when, as the
author writes, "the sea of the soul, heaving
after a calm," gave up its dead. He drove
Hattie from his bed with vile imprecations, sob-

bing the pathetic confession: "You made me do it. And Ah ain't never goin' tuh git over it long ez Ah live."

Hattie divorced John and, in a sense, disgraced him. But she needed further recompense from him. Together with a faction in the church, she arranged a conference at which she could bring charges against the pastor, but the maneuver failed. Later, in a contest with another preacher who had been brought in to try to influence the congregation to issue him to call to the pastorate of Zion Hope, John won big. Using his "Dry Bones" sermon, John brought the church to his side. The other minister gave what the members called a "lecture" as he preached on race pride. Clearly, the author has given the greater weight to the hybrid mixture of the Old Testament and primitive, pre-Christian worship, which, during the sermon, brought his congregation to such a frenzy that it subsided only after two deacons seized John by the arms and reverently set him down. Others rushed up into the pulpit to fan him and wipe his face, declaring, "Dat's uh preachin' piece uh plunder, you hear me?" For their own religious purposes, John Pearson, the poet-preacher, brought to his congregation whatever salvation it expected or wanted. His love affairs, nor the "race pride lecture" of the visiting rival were needed or wanted by the church and its members.

That part of the contest, or the tension, was easy. But the irrepressible difficulty lay in John's own mind. For even in the divorce hearing, his humiliation did not come from the legal separation from Hattie nor from the testimony about his incontinent behavior. He approached a stature akin to heroics--as much as the situation would permit--when he answered that he had no witnesses and would not testify against Hattie. Only when he made this statement did the tittering of his friends and his neighbors and

106

the jibes of the white members of the court end
and their attention was turned abruptly to the
business of issuing the divorce. But the hatred
his enemies held for him and displayed toward
him during the divorce hearing saddened John and
provided for Miss Hurston the opportunity to
make a meaningful statement about the preacher
as leader and community idol:

> The toadies were there.   Armed with
> hammers.   Ever eager to break the feet
> of the fallen idols. Contemptuous that
> even the feet of idols should fall among
> them. No fury so hot as that of synophant
> as he stands above a god that has toppled
> from a shrine.   Faces of gods must not be
> seen of him. He has worshipped beneath
> the feet so long that if a god but lowers
> his face among them, they obscene it with
> spit. "Ha!" they cried, "what kind of a
> divinity is that that levels his face with
> mine? Gods show feet--not faces.   Feet
> that crush--feet that crumble--feet that
> have no eyes for men's suffering nor ears
> for agony, lest indeed it be a sweet
> offering at God's feet.   If gods have no
> power for cruelty, why then worship them?
> Gods tolerate sunshine, but bestir them-
> selves that men may have storms.   From
> the desolation of our fireplaces, let us
> declare the glory.   If he rides upon the
> silver-harnassed donkey, let us cry
> "hosanna." If he weeps in compassion, let
> us lynch him. The sky-rasping mountain-
> peal fills us with awe, but if it tumbles
> in to the valley it is but boulders.   It
> should be burst asunder. Too long it has
> tricked us into worship and filled our
> souls with envy. Crush! Crush! Crush!
> Lord, thou has granted thy servant the
> boon of pounding upon a peak.

Yes, the injury was great. But even in his
fall--even as the toadies attacked with their

hammers and took their one chance to destroy
their God--John Pearson told his friend who
wanted to be called as a witness on his behalf
he did not want the white folks to hear about
anything like that which could be said about
Hattie; for they already knew too much about
Negroes. "Dey's some strings on our harp fuh us
tuh play on and sing all tuh ourselves," he reasoned. Because they thought all Negroes were
ignorant and immoral, they would have not been
surprised at hearing about Hattie's men, he
said. The sad part, to him, was that the white
folks could not tell the difference between a
woman like Hattie and one like Lucy. So he said
nothing.

After having pastored Zion Hope Baptist
Church for 17 years, John preached his last sermon there soon after the divorce, using for his
theme, "The Wounds of Jesus," and basing his remarks on a scriptural passage which expressed
rather well his own heart's agony: "When the
father shall ask, 'What are these wounds in thine
hand?' He shall answer, 'Those are they with
which I was wounded in the house of my freinds."
His long and fervent sermon, rendered in the
novel without dialect elicited a mighty response
from the congregation. It was communion Sunday
and he was expected to serve the sacrament after
preaching, but while the church was in its frenzy, he walked with bowed head out of the church,
telling his friends, "Ah don't b'leive Ah'm
fitted tuh preach de gospel--unless de world is
wrong. Yuh see dey's ready fuh uh preacher tuh
be uh man uhmongst men, but dey ain't ready yet
fuh 'im tuh be uh man uhmongst women." Therefore, he resolved to stay out of the pulpit and
do carpentry for a living.

Out of the pulpit, though, he was a fallen
idol; for the race and the church wanted a
saint and a sinner for a preacher, but it could
not abide an ex-preacher in its midst.

108

His unfavorable changes of fortune caused him to go to another town in which he became married again and again a pastor of a larger church than Zion Hope. His wife was near his own age and loved him dearly; but once more he journeyed to the town in which he had pastored for 17 years-- the town of the death of Lucy and the divorce from Hattie; and once more he spent two hours in a prostitute's arms. On his return home, he was killed by a train which struck his automobile.

One does not conclude reading about John Pearson with a sense of censoring him. Hurston has so mixed the elements of the saint and the sinner in him that one grieves for him, chastizes him, glories in his victories, suffers with his burden of guilt, and--perhaps most of all--thrills to his poetry-making. Perhaps the novel spins out his story over too long a period of time. The last marriage and pastorate seem anticlimactic. But the image of the preacher as presented by Miss Hurston is complex and authentic for the black experience in the Christian practice in America. And, as Hurston stated in the Letter to Johnson, referred to at the beginning of this discussion, one cannot say John Pearson was not a success in the pulpit.

CHAPTER 6 . . . . LANGSTON HUGHES:
            "Big Meetings": Rural and Urban

Langston Hughes (1902-1967) is probably the best-
known black American writer. Having been born in
Joplin, Missouri, he lived with his mother and
other relatives in Lawrence and Topeka in Kansas,
and in Cleveland, Ohio, where he graduated from
high school. He spent the year after his graduation from high school with his father in Mexico
before returning to the United States. He published his first poetry and short fiction in the
black "little" magazines, The Crisis and The
Messenger. After having spent a few years traveling around the world, Hughes returned home and
enrolled at Lincoln University in Pennsylvania.
He received his bachelors degree there in 1929.
Hughes published poetry, fiction, and plays. Some
of his notable works include the poetry collections, The Weary Blues (1926); Fine Clothes to the
Jew (1927); The Dream Keeper and Other Poems (1932);
and Shakespeare in Harlem (1942). Not Without
Laughter (1930) was his first and most popular
novel. Some of his drama has been collected into
Five Plays by Langston Hughes (1963), Webster
Smalley, Editor.

LANGSTON HUGHES: "BIG MEETINGS": RURAL AND URBAN

    Hughes was an enormously prolific writer who
produced works in all of the major literary
genres. One play and two short stories, particularly, focus upon the preacher's relationship to
the community that reacts to what the religious
leader says and does and what others expect of
one who occupies this leadership position. In
each, the preacher is a performer whose roll carries significant implications of the purposes
religion serves in that racial setting. Taken

together, the works cover some thirty years of Hughes' literary career.

In "Big Meeting", the preacher's stylized image is an ingenious characterization in which the ceremonial ritual of an evangelical church service enacts a major ambiguity in the American society. Blacks and whites share a religion. But its images and words carry widely different meanings for the two races. In "Tambourines to Glory" and "Rock Church," the church has come to the city and the preacher reflects the tensions of urban life as they press upon personal aspiration and economic pressures. In these settings the social and political statements are more diffuse than those that issue from the pastoral setting of the rural South. Accordingly, the moral imperatives become more complex and the image of the preacher moves from dignified performance into grotesque machinations that issue from several levels of personal frustration.

Each work speaks significantly about the black American and his religion, not as a scientist or a theologian would view it, but within the powerful vision of a black creative artist whose basic material is the collected memory of the race.

"Big Meeting"

Twelfth Night concluded the Christmas festivities in the medieval world, and marked the feast commemorating the coming of the Magi as the first manifestation of Christ to the Gentiles. Hughes' short story, "Big Meeting," loosely parallels the medieval tradition and restates the custom as ironic comedy. Its plot is laid in the twelfth night of the conventional revival meeting in a small Southern town. The Reverend Duke Braswell, the true Master of the Revelries, convincingly teaches the "Magi"--the white power structure of the community--the real meaning of Christianity.

In his performance as guest preacher who has come "from afar," he challenges the social values of the town in sound and sight of those who rule there. Braswell is an outsider, in the primary sense, but he is also the powerful chief spokesman of the lore, poetry, and religious truth of the black community. In the story he shows an understanding of the essence of Christianity that is infinitely superior to that held by those who taught him and his ancestors about Jesus Christ. In Hughes' hands, Braswell becomes the public teacher who brings a lesson in Christianity to anyone who is able and willing to be taught the truth that he represents in his natural performance, without using a single word or gesture that he would not use to his black audience.

This twelfth night of the big meeting, the unnamed teenage narrator and his friend Bud joined the procession of "a great many Negroes, old and young," who plodded down the dirt road on foot to the big tent, lighted by lanterns, where early arrivals were already clapping their hands lustily as they sang the age-old congs of their religion. Through the eyes and feelings of these two young black boys, one gets the strained sense of community the revival fosters. For in the road that ran past the woods, automobiles and buggies belonging to white people had stopped near the tent to listen to the singing. Whites indicated a self-conscious separation of the races as they stared curiously through the hickory trees at the rocking figures in the tent. The two young boys were at least superficially detached from the revival, too; "we were young and wild in those days, and didn't believe in revivals, anyhow, so we stayed outside in the road where we could smile and laugh like the white folks" the narrator explains. But the boys maintained a tie with the inside of the tent. Their mothers were there. Through the boys the reader learns the format for Big Meetings:

From the frequent attendance since child-

hood at these Big Meetings, held each
summer, we knew that the services were
divided into three parts. The testimonials and the song service came first.
This began as soon as two or three people
were gathered together, continuing until
the minister himself arrived. Then the
sermon followed, with its accompanying
songs and shouts from the audience. Then
the climax came with the calling of the
lost souls to the mourners bench, and the
prayers for sinners and backsliders. And
this was where Bud and I would leave. We
were having too good a time being sinners,
and we didn't want to be saved--not yet,
anyway.

That night as the crowd grew large, Bud and
his friend watched closely, "keeping our eyes
open for the girls"; but they sat outside, al-
lying themselves, superficially, with the whites
who watched and listened from their cars. "Sometimes there would be as many as ten or twelve
parties of whites parked out there in the dark,
smoking and listening, and enjoying themselves. . .in a not very serious way," the reader
learns. Mr. Parkes, the owner of the drugstore
where colored people could not buy a glass of
soda at the fountain, arrived with his date:

"You'll hear some good singing out there,"
Mr. Parkes said to the lady in the car with
him.

"I always did love to hear darkies singing,"
she answered from the back seat.

Bud nudged me in the ribs at the word darkie.

"I hear 'em," I said, sitting down on one
of the gnarled roots of the tree and pulling
out a cigarette.

Inside, the testifying had begun. One woman addressed the congregation:

I rise to testify dis evenin' fo' Jesus!
He's ma Savior an' ma Redeemer an de cham-
ber wherin I resuscitates my soul. Pray
fo; me, brothers and sisters. Let yo'
mercies bless me in all I do an' yo'
prayers with me on each travellin' voyage!

Another sang in a clear soprano voice:

I am a po' pilgrim of sorrow
Out in this wide world alone. . . .

Many others joined her and sang:

Sometimes I am tossed and driven,
Sometimes I don't know where to go. . . .

"Real pretty, ain't it?" the white woman remarked to Parkes. When the black woman rose to
testify, she told how her husband had left her
with six little children, her mother had died in
the poorhouse, the white woman half-laughed, "My,
she's had a hard time." "Sure has, to hear her
tell it," Parkes agreed. The black woman warmed
up to reciting her tribulations, ending with:
"White folks and devils beset me--but I'm goin'
on"; and men and women sanctioned her testimony
and her determination. Already, what Parkes and
his lady friend had said erased some of the arti-
ficial separation between the young boys and the
activities inside the tent. The narrators described his mother's entrance into the fervor of
the common experiences of the elders:

Rocking proudly to and fro the second
chorus boomed and swelled beneath the canvas, mama began to clap her hands, her own
lips silent now in this second song she had
started, her head thrown back in joy--for
mama was a great shouter. Stepping grace-
fully to the beat of the music, she moved

115

out toward the center aisle into a cleared
space. Then she began to spring on her toes
with little short rhythmical hops. All the
way up the long aisle to the pulpit gently
she leaped to the clap-clap of hands, the
pat of feet, and the steady booming song
of her fellow worshippers. Then mama
began to revolve in a dignified circle,
slowly, as a great happiness swept her
gleaming black features, and her lips
curved into a smile.

I've opened up to heaven all de windows
    of my soul. . . .
Mama was dancing, dancing before the Lord
with her eyes closed, her mouth smiling,
and her head held up high.

Now I'm livin' on de halleluia side!
And as she danced she threw her hands upward, away from her breasts, as though she
were casting off the cares of the world.

    "My Lord, John, just look at the niggers
shouting! It's better than a show," one white woman exclaimed and her words made the narrator's
blood boil. That was his mother standing up
shouting. Maybe it was funny, maybe it was better
than a show, but no white folks had any business
laughing at her. If his mother thought there was
something better in heaven than white folks gave
her on earth, what business did they have laughing at her? He and Bud laughed and made fun of
the shouters often, but deep down inside themselves, they loved their mothers and sympathized
with their plight and understood why they came to
the Big Meeting. Working all day all their lives
for white folks, disappointed and poor, bossed and
underpaid, no wonder they wanted to fool themselves into believing in Heaven. Perhaps his own
mother was grotesque and old and foolish, but
what could she do other than find release from
the cares of the day by singing about a never-to-
be-realized hope?

116

As the narrator feels most helpless and most
unified to those of his heritage he may seem to
deny, the skillfully written story introduces the
prophet, poet, and priest who--not in a single act
but in a massive sweep of hope and beauty--can do
what no one else in the world can do. For even
while the best of songs, congregational prayers,
pathetic testimonials have been offered, it is the
Reverend Duke Braswell who arrives to cap the
highest possible emotional experience. He steps
to the pulpit:

> A tall, powerful, jet-black man with a head
> like a giant, he moved up the aisle. With
> long steps through the center of the tent
> he strode, his woolly iron-gray hair un-
> covered, his green-black preacher's coat
> reaching to his knees, and his fierce eyes
> looking straight toward the altar. Under
> his arm he carried a Bible.

> Once on the platform, he stood silently
> wiping his brow with a large white hand-
> kerchief while the singing swirled about
> him. Then he sang, too, his voice roaring
> above the others, his white teeth shining,
> his big mouth red inside. Finally he held
> up his palms for silence and the people
> gradually began to hum, hum, hum, hands and
> feet still patting, bodies still moving--
> but at last, above the undertones of song
> and the broken cries of shouters, he was
> able to make himself heard.

> "Praise God, Brothers and Sisters, I believe
> I'm on that halleluia side!. . . Amen! . . .
> a prayer."

When a hymn he had ordered a sister to begin
had ended and while the congregation still hummed,
the preacher took his text from the open Bible:
"Ye now therefore have sorrow; but I will see you
again, and your hearts shall rejoice, and your
joy <u>no</u> man taketh from you." The big black man

117

slammed shut the holy book and walked to the edge
of the pulpit—and spoke to his waiting congregation: "That's what Jesus said befo' he went to
de cross, children--I will see you agin, an' yo'
hearts shall rejoice."

And he told the familiar story of the death
of Jesus as he stood there in the dim light of the
smoking oil lanterns. Power without money, titles
or position, he called Jesus' power over the mul-
titudes--a power that went out to the poor and
afflicted. For Jesus said, "the first shall be
last and the last shall be first." This quota-
tion allied the black congregation--and, indeed,
the black race--to Christianity, and the preacher
enunciated that relationship in full hearing of
the teenage boys and the cynics outside. He
possessed the unique power; he propitiated the
imbalance between white and black people. In his
identification with the power in Jesus Christ,
the preacher rendered his people equal, if not
superior, to those who exploited them and found
their religion a comical and entertaining cine-
cure. He became Master of the Revelries within
the highest tradition of the nation's ethics. To
all the black people--the boys and congregation--
he was Jesus Christ for a moment. Through his
role as story-teller and interpolator, he became
a transubstantiation of the essence of Christ.
He related with dignity and authority the details
of the life of Christ in those most essential portions of the Christian religion--the betrayal in
the garden and the Crucifixion. Religion became
a mystical experience for him and his audience as
he united those icons of the Christian religion
to the life experience of his own people. Re-
telling the myths became reality for his hearers
as he thundered:

Then de big people o' de land heard about
Jesus, . . .the chief priests an'de scribes,
de politicians, de bootleggers, an de bank-
ers--an' they begun to conspire against
Jesus because He had Power! This Jesus with

118

His twelve disciples walkin' and preachin'
in Galilee. . . . Then came that eve o' de
Passover, when he set down with His friends
to ean an' drink o' de wine as de settin'
sun fell behind de hills o' Jerusalem. An'
Jesus knew then that ere de cosk crew Judas
would betray him, an' Peter would say, 'I
know him not," an' all alone by hisself He
would go to His death. Yes, sir, he knew!
So He got up from de table an' went into de
garden to pray. In this hour o' trouble
Jesus went to pray!

As his prelude to the Crucifixion rolled off
the tongue of the preacher, he described the tragedy of the Garden Gethsemane in terms that com-
municated with his black congregation: "the mob";
the handcuffs; the disciples who fled because they
were afraid; the chains; the trial; Peter's denial. The darkened pity and horror of the im-
pending death of Jesus Christ filled the air:

The preacher chanted, half-moaning his sentences, not speaking them now. His breath
came in quick, short gasps with an indrawn,
"Umn!" between each rapid phrase. Perspiration poured down his shiny black face as
he strode across the platform wrapped in
this drama that he saw in the very air
before his eyes. Peering over the heads of
his audience and out into the darkness, he
began the ascent to Golgotha, describing
the taunting crowd at Christ's heels and
the heavy cross on His shoulders.

The preacher embellished the narrative of the
actual nailing of Jesus to the cross as his tour
de force. "They brought de nails, four long iron
nails, an' they put one in de palm of His left
hand. An' de hammer said. . .Bam! . . .An' they
put one in de palm of His right hand. An' de
hammer said. . .Bam! . . .An' they put one through
His left foot. . .Bam! . . ." With this personal
and ingenious method of delivery, his audience

119

shrieked back, "Don't drive it! Oh! for Christ's sake. Don't drive it!" But the Reverend Braswell continued with his methodically graphic description of the Crucifixion until his words fell upon the ultimate association between the black man and Jesus: "They stoned Him first. They called Him everything but a chile o' God. Then they lynched Him on the cross." He and the congregation move then in a common knowledge and sense of the use of the materials of worship in their own view of Christianity as an old woman led in singing "Were You There When They Crucified My Lord?" The preacher and everyone joined it now. At this moment of denouement, no hands clapped; no bodies swayed; on the screens of their own minds, everyone in the tent pictured the tremendous death of Christ. The Reverend Duke Braswell stretched wide his arms against the white canvas of the tent, and in the yellow lantern light his body made a great crosslike shadow.

"Let's go," said the white woman with Mr. Parkes, "that's too much for me!" "It's time for you to go," the narrator called out loud from his seat around the root of a tree. "They're about to call for sinners--to come and be saved."

The dramatic sermon has unified all persons who can become one with the religious experience the revival represents. Two teenage boys can appear to reject its value; they can remain outside so long as they kept out of sight of their mothers. They were not ready to "stop sinning," they say. But the superficial cleavage which they believe separates them from the experience of their parents and their peers melted when the white outsiders who have come for entertainment, ridicule the shouting women inside.

The image of the preacher, though, stands paramount in this powerful story. For in his art as preacher, he argues the black man's case with deadly effectiveness. He proves that the suffering of the poor black person in the United States

represents a legitimate claim to the vitality of
Christianity which no other American can claim so
clearly. The suffering establishes and maintains
the link. If Christianity is a defensible religion for the nation, black men merit the power
and the glory of the nation. White men who come
out every year to find entertainment in observing
the revival at a distance become eventually im-
mune to its gravity. The white woman who is with
Mr. Parkes, though must be unfamiliar with the
services. She actually hears and sees the black
experience the revival meeting illustrates. She
hears people tell their troubles to their fellowmen in public and without restraint. She sees
the women--black women, however--who dance and
sing their religion with earnestness and abandon.
Her response to these actions is humorous ridicule. At best, she is amused. But when the story
of Jesus Christ--her Jesus Christ--is told in
moving and graphic detail, even to the point of
the silhouette of Her Jesus Christ reflected on
the tent's canvas by this extremely black man,
"that's too much for me!" she exclaimed. On the
terms of the narrator she had no choice but to
run to the mourner's bench and confess her personal and corporate sins. But she could never
make that decision. So, she must get out of hearing and sight of that which earlier in the evening had seemed amusing, even if ludicrous.

The preacher, then, becomes the medium that
teaches morality to the race's oppressors, and
he teaches it on the oppressor's own terms. His
earnestness, his dignity, his thundering poetry
deserve respectful hearing. And it troubles the
hearer. The effectiveness of this particualr
image of the preacher provides at least two levels
of unity: The black younger generation with the
older and also the white with the black. In the
former circumstance, common view of meaning of
Jesus Christ fosters unity. In the latter, the
potential exists, but the motivation remains impossible. Yet, the sincere and authentic practice
of religion as illustrated by "Big Meeting" finds

121

full approval with the author, through his spokesman as the teenage narrator, primarily. But, the
magic-maker is the Reverand Duke Braswell who di-
rects and motivates the social statement of the
story and who provides an opportunity for Epiphany
for the Magi of the community in which the story
is set.

"Tambourines to Glory"

Hughes called "Tambourines: a fable, a folk
ballad in stage form, told in broad and simple
terms about problems that can only convincingly
be reduced to a comic trip if presented "cleanly,
clearly, sharply, precisely and with humor." But
the plot is not humorous. As comedy it holds up
the mirror to an unsavory part of Nature. The unfolding drama brings salvation and redemption to
characters worthy of saving. They are the two
women who represent the duality of saint and sinner in the black preacher. The tension in "Tambourines" brings them full circle from the beginning of their spurious religious venture into full
reconciliation by the final curtain. As a morality play "Tambourines" executes a struggle between
good and evil and signifies some complications
that can arise when absolute evil consumes the
means and emotions of human fallibility. The play
contains the time-honored issues of the human condition. Its value system excoriates the syco-
phants on the streets of Harlem and in the city
government downtown who freely enter the operation
of the church of the simple folk to exploit them
and perpetrate a more devastating and widespread
diablerie than conventional storefront preachers
could carry out without the motivation of professional manipulators. The frightening needs of
the street people, brought on by their economic
plight, provide the efficient cause for their exploitation. But the ethic of the drama does not
reject an institution that offers hope to destitute members who flock to churches. It simply
roots out, as it unfolds, the malevolence that

subverts potentially good purposes the simple church can serve.

Laura Wright Reed and Essie Belle Jackson begin their church to solve their economic crisis. The first scene of the play opens on a Harlem street one spring night. Essie has been evicted from her tenement room and her belongings are piled on the curb. She is sitting on one of her suitcases as passers-by turn to look at her plight. A teenager who stops to look at her inquires what happened. "Evicted, that's all," she replies. "Damn! Ain't that enough?" asks the youth. Essie, providing the first clue to her character, retorts, "No use to to use profanity, son." The youth answers, "Excuse me, m'am. But I still say damn!" A woman stops to sympathize and asks whether Essie will sit on the curb all night. "I reckon God'll provide for me. My credit's run out," Essie explains. She has no relatives in New York; she was married once to a man who was not much good; she is alone. Within a few lines of the play, Essie's plight, as determined largely by economics, has been established. Laura, a kindly prostitute and friend, threatens to move Essie back into the building. Learning that the marshall has padlocked the door, Laura considers ways she may help her dispossessed friend: "Essie, you can move in with me for the night. But, you know, I got too many boy friends to be having a permanent guest. I told you, you ought to get on relief like me. Essie, get yourself a man." Instead of doing something to solve her problem, Essie is just "setting looking peaceful," Laura tells her when she ought to be raising hell. The tension between personalities of the two women-- one "setting looking peaceful" and the other raising hell--becomes the philosophical basis for the distinctions between them and the duality of the character of the black preacher Hughes portrays in this work, as the following dialogue illustrates:

Essie: About all I can do, Laura, is ask

the Lord to take my hand.

Laura: Why don't you do that then? Get
holy, sanctify yourself--since
we're setting out here on the
curb discussing the ways and means.
The Lord is no respector of persons--
if He takes the pimp's hand and makes
a bishop out of him. You know Bishop
Longjohn right over there on Lenox
Avenue? That saint had three whores
on the block ten years ago. He's
got a better racket now--the gospel!
And a rock and roll band in front of
the pulpit.

Essie: Religion don't have to be a racket,
Laura. Do it? Maybe he's converted.

Laura: The money he takes in every Sunday
would convert me. Say, I got an
idea! Why don't you and me start a
church?

Essie: What denomination?

Laura: Our own then we won't be beholding to
nobody else. You know my grandpa was
a jackleg preacher, so I can rock a
church as good as anybody.

Essie: Did you ever preach?

Laura: No, but I've got the nerve to try.
Let's start a church. Huh?

Essie: Where?

Laura: On the street where the Bishop started
his--outdoors--rent free--on the corner.

Essie: You mean down here in the gutter
         where I am?

Laura: On the curb--_above_ the gutter.
         We'll save them lower down than us.

When Essie asks who could be lower down than
she is at the moment, Laura tells her those who
do what she cannot do: drink without getting drunk;
gamble away their rent; cheat the Welfare Department; lay with each other without getting disgusted; blow guage and support the dope trade;
hustle. They are the ones the church will set out
to convert with the Lord Jesus Christ who comes
free, Laura explains. "Just look up at the Lord
above and the squares will think God is staring
you dead in the face," and what is more, "we'll
make money's mammy!" Essie is not convinced that
making money is that easy. She has always had
bad luck. She has not been able to have her 16-
year-old daughter with her two continuous years
since she has been born. Laura does not believe
in bad luck. She is the personification of action
and expediency who needs someone like Essie to
work with in the new project. So she pushes the
establishment of the church along with the challenge:

Essie, raise you fat and disgusted self up
off that suitcase you're setting on and let's
go make our fortunes saving souls. Remember
that white woman, that Aimee Semple McPherson
what put herself on some wings, opened a
temple, and made a million dollars? Girl,
we'll call ourselves sisters--use my name--
the Reed Sisters--even if ain't no relation--
sisters in God. I preach and you sing. We'll
let the sinners in the gutter come to us.
Listen to my spiel. I can shoop and holler
real good. (She mounts a pile of furniture
imagining herself a preacher.) I'll tell them
Lenox Avenue Sinners: You all better come to
Jesus! The atom bomb's about to destroy this
world and you ain't ready. Get ready! Get ready!

"Broke as we are, we better start a church,"
she tells Essie how they can begin such a project.
The answer is simple to the ebullient Laura who
remembers that she had dreamt of fish during her
afternoon nap. She believes the number for fish
is 782 and asks Essie for fifty cents to play that
number. Essie warns that her friend should be
thinking of praying, not playing, but she contrib-
utes the quarter she has and Laura promises that
if 782 "comes out," she will put half of what she
wins down on a Bible. In a highly theatrical, but
appropriate action which approaches apothesis,
Essie suddenly rises, looking upward, and exclaims,
"Laura, I just got a vision. A voice tells me to
take you up on this--and try to save you, too."
As Laura stares with amazement, Essie, her face
flooded with radiance, mounts her pile of furniture and sings of the church she will build upon
the rock of her faith, at the same time snatching
from Laura the wine bottle and throwing it away,
as the two of them fall in to the spirit of
Essie's vision and resolve.

A meaningful epiphany of the community, led
jointly by Essie and Laura, takes place on the
street of Harlem as the women dramatically cry out
their call which has come and their determination
to heed it with the establishment of the church.
The sense of the community and its participation
in the revelation become evident as windows open,
heads pop out, a few passers-by stop to watch and
listen. A few more gather, and as the scene ends
the crowd which has gathered reflects the archi-
typal nature of the communal religious perception
into which Essie and Laura have led them as they
all sing:

> Amen! Hallelujah! Bless God! Yes! Amen!
>   Amen!
> I say, oh, yes! I build my church!
> The gates of hell shall not prevail.
> Upon this rock I build my church!
> In God's own grace, I shall not fail.

Significantly in the ethic of Langston Hughes'
racial vision--particularly with respect to its
religious dimensions--a ministry, a church, and a
congregation have risen from sources which appear
only slightly related to conventional and formal
considerations of religion: economic necessity on
Essie's part, tempered with a stubborn sense of
what is appropriate in Christianity; disenchant-
ment with boring men she must deal with in pros-
titution; memory of a grandfather who was a preacher of sorts; and recognition of the successes
which a white woman--Aimee Semple McPherson--had
experienced in establishing a specious religion of
her own, motivated Laura. Racial memory, quick-
ened in the neighbors by incantations from the
Scriptures recited by Essie and Laura in a loud
voice under their windows and in their midst on
the curb, establishes religion, church, and
preacher. Economic destitution binds the preachers to their present and potential congregation,
giving substance to the author's biting statement
that these conditions, whenever and wherever they
come together with appropriate quantity and quality, create the religious community, the religious
contours, and the religious form of practice. Exploitation is not the exclusive domain of those
who live in Harlem, as the example of Aimee Semple
McPherson makes known. Given a ministry which,
in this case, contains the conventional respect
for her religious tradition which Essie tries to
maintain through her questions about the propri-
ety of beginning a church simply because she and
Laura want one, fused with the element of Laura
which honestly states that the purpose for such a
project is purely monetary, one finds in "Tambourines" the opportunity to observe clearly this
duality in the image of the preacher.

How the counterplot of their purposes trans-
lates itself into their actions as preachers appears first early in scene two, as the communal
experience of the neighborhood fades into a di-
minishing reprise and from the ether of group
thinking, feeling, and action emerge Essie and

Laura with their church established but not secured. Essie, predictably, continues to pray,
"Grant us your grace, Jesus! Fill us with thy
word, Lord, and bless this corner on which we,
your humble servants, stand tonight," but earthy
and efficient Laura realizes they need an audience. "Ain't nobody paying you no attention,"
she tells Essie, as the burst of fervor from the
community subsides. Moving through the crowd,
shaking her tambourine, Laura moves in to hustle
the street people. "Aw, Lady, Hush!" someone
cries out when Essie calls for sinners. Laura,
seeing them slow to respond, moves into telling a
dramatic, but deliberate, lie that she knows will
attract attention. It comes from the black community's collected experience with religion:

> Yes, you sinners, I say stop! Stop in your
> tracks now and listen to my words. (As she
> speaks gradually a crowd gathers.) Lemme
> tell you how I got the call. It was one
> night last spring with Sister Essie here,
> right on the street, I saw a flash, I heard
> a roll of thunder, I felt a breeze and I
> seen a light and a voice exploding out of
> heaven cried, "Laura Wright Reed," it said,
> "Take up the Cross and follow Me!" Oh, yes,
> that voice said, told me to come out on this
> corner tonight and save you! You young man
> laughing and about to pass on by. Stop!
> Stop and listen to my word. "Take up the
> Cross," it said, "and follow Me. Get out
> into the highways and byways and save souls.
> Go to the curbstones and gutters," it said,
> "rescue the lost. Approach." I was told,
> "approach the river of sin and pull out the
> drowning, brothers and sisters, just like you,
> until I got saved. I were down there too,
> in sin's gutter, lower than a snake's belly--
> now look at me up here on the curbstone of
> life reaching out to you to come and be saved.

No one contradicts Laura's wildly concocted
story, although many persons on the street might

128

well remember how the two women actually started
preaching. Now, the church has been established
on the street corner. "Our roof is God's sky--
there is no door," Laura exclaims and the simple,
pastoral description, even on a busy Harlem corner, finds support among persons whose images of
religion and preachers are like Laura's. They
begin to drop nickels, dimes, and quarters into
the tambourine and, along with the women preachers, they sing the songs of the religion they all
know in common. To those who refuse to pitch a
coin into the collection, Laura says, "you can't
get saved for nothing." C.J., a young guitar
player has joined them. Laura says the Lord has
sent him to make up songs for his glory rather
than playing rock and roll.

One night, while the crowd is singing the song
of communal approbation, "Upon this rock I build
my church," a policeman emerges and calls quietly,
"Say, listen, you women." Appropriate to her own
earthy sensibilities and experiences, Laura says
to the policeman, for the benefit of the audience,
"I'll see you later, Mister Law. Let us sing
God's songs." But aside, she whispers, "Don't
worry man, just be cool. Be cool." When the
verse ends and while Essie is still singing with
the crowd, Laura slips money to the policeman with
the explanation, "As long as you let us get ours,
baby, you'll get yours." The policeman warns her
that she really should get a license if she is
going to sing on the street every night, and Laura
reminds him that he is getting paid and that
should be sufficient for him. What she is paying
will do him, he admits, but it will not satisfy
the brass downtown. Laura tells him they, too,
can be bought. The deeper and wider and stronger
evil that will significantly affect the church has
appeared, but Laura, despite her worldliness, does
at this point understand the level of manipulation she has entered.

To this point, exploitation has been minimal.
Essie and Laura have established their church in

order to make a lining for themselves they cannot make as easily in any other way. The community has joined willingly and out of identification
with the collected consciousness among them and
the preachers. They gave money because of their
traditional belief that their gifts would merit
favors from God. The suggestion of evil has been
made in Laura's attitude toward the project in
comparison with Essie's. Forthcoming elements in
the unfolding of the plot indicate degrees and
levels of evil; that the willingness of the
preachers and the neighborhood to work together
in a mutually beneficial religious experience is
one thing, but that the intrusion of outside
forces for <u>purely</u> one-sided official exploitation
is quite a different and far more serious problem.
Thus, the introduction of the policeman who can
be paid by Laura without her even bothering to
mention his demand to Essie quickly leads to the
major force of evil in terms of the play's ethic.

Good-looking, Big-Eyed Buddy Lomax enters. He
is the hustler who preys upon the sinner side of
Laura, whets her carnal desire, and links his
victimization of the church to the larger official
manipulation from downtown. This forte possesses
resources that can permit lures and a leisurely
pace overwhelming by many times the motivations
and hustling of the preachers who live off the
community and the policeman who makes extra
money off petty law breakers. Buddy Lomax represents villainy. He is the major embodiement of
evil in the drama. In the Prologue he has introduced himself appropriately:

You think I am who you see, don't you?
Well, I'm not. I'm the devil. In this
play, according to the program, you
might think I'm Big-Eyed Buddy Lomax--
if I didn't tell you in front, no, I'm
not. Big-Eyed Buddy is just <u>one</u> of my
million and one names. I've <u>got</u> plenty
of names, had plenty of big ones--Hitler,
for example. Yes, Hitler was me! Mack-

130

the-Knife, Gyp-the-Blood, Don Juan among
the covers. Oh, yes! Henry the Eighth.
Katherine the Great--I put on drag sometimes. Iago. Brutus--et tu, Brute--right
on back to Cain. Little names, big names--
I'm liable to have your name. . . . The
Devil comes in various guises--and dis-
guises. I'm disguised now. I am not the
me you see here--tall, handsome, brownskin. I am not always dark--sometimes I'm
white. Sometimes yellow, sometimes Krushchev.
I speak all tongues. . . all languages are
mine. In Harlem, I'm cool, in Spain, I'm
hot. . . . Sure, I have my troubles, get shot
up once in a while, ambushed, assassinated.
But, quiet as it's kept, I love being the
Devil because I raise so much hell! . . . .
On this stage you'll see sin and salvation,
me and God, Beelzebub and Jehovah wrestling
one more time. The old struggle between
sanctity and Satan, the Christians and the
damned! The, damned, that's me. I never
win--but I have a hell of a good time trying.
And I'm generous. I'll even let the good
church folks have a head start. . . .

Yet, he is only the Harlem link to absolute,
official evil. He is the black representative of
downtown--the one who can ingratiate himself with
minor crime to keep inviolate the true power
sources. The money Laura and Essie are collecting
from their church on the street corner is mere pea-
nuts to him. Moreover, winter is coming and the
church will cease. The alternative is for it to
move indoors. Laura complains about the high rent
she would have to pay for a storefront and Buddy
tempts her with the promise of helping her to
build Tambourine Temple. Marty, the invisible
power downtown, will sponsor the enterprise.
Laura's vanity overpowers her good sense and she
becomes Buddy's willing pupil as he teaches her
sophisticated ways to extract real money from her
followers. He tells her that once she gets her
own temple she can sell holy water from the Jordan

131

River. When Laura asks naively how much it would cost to import the water into the country, Buddy tells her, "Turn on the tap, that's all. For little or nothing I can get you a hundred gross of empty bottles with labels on them." He can paste green labels that say "HOLY WATER" on bottles about the size of small Listerine containers and she can "just take them to the sink" and fill them with the water she can sell during the church services. Fascinated, Laura asks whether he is talking about water which was not really holy and he answers, "It's holy if you bless it, Sister Laura." She likes the idea and they agree to sell the Holy Water for a dollar a bottle. With the bottle and the label costing about two cents and the water free, they could see a Cadillac by Christmas. But who is Marty? Buddy tells her he is the fixer—the man behind the men behind the men who can get you anything. Is he colored? she wanted to know. "You know he can't be colored," Buddy answers.

Essie wanted a church which could do good things for Harlem—playgrounds for children, employment office, day nursery for the children of working mothers. She wanted to get herself some good clothes in good time, but first she wanted to have a good church. "The needs is so big up here in harlem, we have to do all we can, me and you," she told Laura, "and you're God's handmaiden, even if you don't always act like a holy maiden do." She did not like Laura's public lovemaking with Buddy, and she had never accepted the Holy Water confidence game. "I'm gonna live fine, and look fine," Laura hurls back at Essie, and the duality comes again into focus with the conflict within its elements:

> Essie: Laura, one of these days the spirit is going to strike vanity from your heart, lust from your body, and. . . .

> Laura: And make me as stupid as you are, heh? Without an idea in your head

                    until I put one there! Without
                    me you'd be still on relief. Yet
                    you want to cramp my style. Well,
                    you won't. I'll tell you now, Essie,
                    I'm getting a fur coat, a Cadillac,
                    and buying a hi-fi set for Buddy.

     They were making good money, Laura told Essie,
and with running five nights a week and taking in
two hundred dollars a night from overflowing
crowds, they would have to move soon into larger
quarters. They were turning all of the old the-
aters in Harlem into churches, she said, and Marty
could rent one for them. And who was this Marty,
Essie asks? You'd think he was the devil and
Buddy his shadow in the form of a snake, Laura
confessed, but she was not afraid of devils. She
had wrestled them all of her life, and some devils
had diamonds in their heads. But she was not taking all of the good things from the church, neither were Buddy and Marty; Essie could have the
money to send for her daughter. Essie was grateful. Laura fought with Buddy, the Devil, when he
tired of her and treated her as any hustler treats
his prey. With her pride hurt because of his bold
flirtations with younger women in her presence and
his insulting reminders that she was too old to
interest him further, the vanity in her heart and
the lust in her body which Essie warned her about,
led Laura to kill Buddy in self-defense. But she
stabbed him with Essie's knife which had been
spoken of throughout the play. Ironically, Essie
was arrested for the murder on the premise that
Buddy's flirtations with her younger daughter,
Marietta, had been the motive. Essie went to her
jail cell naively singing and clasping her Bible.
Her own simple faith and basic goodness, as con-
trasted with Laura's perception of her own role
as preacher, may be illustrated again in the following dialogue between Essie and Crow who has
come to visit the jail cell to inform Essie that
Laura has confessed the murder:

133

Crow: Put your mind at rest, Sister Essie.
         The Lord has already this morning
         give us glad tidings. You gonna get
         out of this mess. The church has
         got you and Sister Laura the best
         lawyers in town. But the big news
         is, Sister Laura confessed--

Essie: Confessed?

Crow: That she killed Buddy Lomax. She
         prayed all night and confessed all
         morning and nobody made her.

Essie: Poor Laura! Now she'll be behind
         bars.

Crow: I been behind bars fifty times. It
         ain't so bad.

Essie: This is my first time, and I sweated
         blood. But I guess if Jesus could
         stand what was done to Him, I can
         stand this mite of punishment vis-
         ited on me. Deacon Crow, I deserve
         this punishment. When I seen what
         was happening in our church--all that
         unholy water selling, numbers and
         stuff--I should have riz in my wrath
         and cleaned house. But no! Instead
         I just set and sung. That's what's
         been the matter with me all these
         years--setting, just setting--accept-
         ing what comes, receiving the Lord's
         blessings whilst the eagle foulest
         his nest--until he gets stuck in the
         back with my own knife.

When Crow tries to interrupt her, she continues, with excitement and determination:

         It don't do to just set. Me, I let
         Buddy fill the house of God with sin,
         let vanities take over, let Laura

parade her fur coats before them
poor peoples what brought us their
hard-earned money for God's work.
Me, I let our church become the
devil's playground. Religion's got
no business being made into a gyp
game. That part of God that is in
anybody is not to be played with--
and everybody has got a part of God
in them. I let Laura play with God.
Me, Essie Belle Johnson. . . . From
here on in, I, Essie Belle Johnson,
am gonna run my church. And I'm
gonna make it what I visioned--a Rock
of Goodness in the heart of Harlem.
We's a wealth church now. I'm gonna
buy that old building next door. . .
and turn that vacant lot into a playground. . . .

When Laura was led into the cell to see Essie
she wept, "Forgive me--after what I did to you."
Essie agreed whe would forgive her and pray for
her.

Tambourine Tmeple was brighter than ever--lit-
erally a blaze of light--when Essie, in charge of
her church, told the congregation God moves in
mysterious ways; that Laura's lawyers had argued
successfully and secured the determination that
Buddy had been slain in self-defense. Most importantly, she shared with them the newspapers
which she said were full of how the end of Buddy
Lomax had unearthed a cesspool of crime in New
York City and the nation--a syndicate with pay-
offs from the corner candy store that writes num-
bers, right on up to the cornerstone of government that protects the martyrs of the underworld.
When she presented her fellow preacher, she referred to her as "repentant--and with head bowed
down--ready to serve years up the river." Laura
spoke to the congregation and confessed that she
had sinned. "Church, I know my punishment is
coming, got to come," she told them, but she was

135

grateful that she was back for the moment with her friends. Her anguish turns into song, as she details the nature of the manner in which she had offended God:

> Mine was a sumptuous kind of sin
> Wrapped in diamonds and fur,
> Scattered money to the wind
> Like frankincense and myrrh.
> Mine was a giddy kind of sin,
> Laughing without care
> While others in this world I knew
> Found no happiness anywhere.
> Mine was lustful kind of sin
> Close, close in lustful arms.
> Mine was hungry kind of sin,
> Hungry for the body's charm--
> Not stopping, no, not thinking
> Of another's harms. . . .
> The harms I brought to one who prayed
> That I might know God's way.
> The very ones who trusted me
> Oh, God, I did betray. . . .

As she begs the church to pray for her--not that she should not go to prison but that she might be forgiven her sins--the crowd answers back again and again, "We'll pray! Got to pray! Must pray!" When she asks whether she can find her way back to salvation with the audience by praying with them for herself, it is Essie who gives her the assurance of pardon:

> Laura, you can. Church, in the name of His charity and His forgiveness, I request Sister Mattie now to place upon this come-home-again lamb, her robe. Help her Sisters, that she might be robed in the love of this Church.

The ritual of the confession and the forgiveness is equally as complete as has been the archetypal religious celebration at the beginning of the church which came into being from deep inside the racial experience of the community,

136

having been struck by Laura and Essie. That same
community joined with Laura in her prayer of con-
trition and in the act of forgiveness. Her non-
self conscious recital of her sins by their own
names returned her to a one-ness with the lack of
malice and the spiritual expectation which the
neighbors had given freely when she had preached
among them. Theirs' is a society of basic love,
understanding, and acceptance of the human side
of even its saints. The unforgivable sin, among
them, represents that which Buddy Lomax and his
Marty impose upon them. They are unable to be
included in the new alignment which has been
worked out through the unfolding of the play.
Buddy has been killed. Laura must pay for killing him, but her penalty must be minimal; for
while she is responsible for her actions in his
death, she has actually excoriated the embodiment
from the society which has already been formed as
the church.

The two sides of the preacher--seeming anti-
thetical--are not irreconcilable. Vanity and
lust lie deep in the heritage of the preacher,
as well as in any other person. Of themselves,
these human qualities are not condemnation. They
are to be watched, controlled; and when they
overcome human beings, they are to be forgiven.
Simple suffering, keeping the faith, renouncing
acts of excess, feeling and working toward the
higher and larger social good--all these attributes and acts of behavior, as exemplified by
Essie--make up the other side of the preacher.
They are the everlasting virtues that can actually wrestle with the devils. Flambouyance, of
itself, is not sinful; for the glory of the song
and the sound of musical instruments and the
cries of joy and of anguish in the human voice
make up the materials of the rituals of the
religious experience. And these rituals are far
from empty. Flambouyance, though, may pave the
way toward degradation, but the other side of the
personality of the preacher is always there to
exert its force on the worship of the flashy

clothes and the plush apartments and the Cad-
illacs and the rock and roll music. That simple
sanity wins finally; for as Buddy in his role as
Devil had told the reader in the Prologue, the
Devil always loses, even if he has a hell of a
lot of fun before he loses. Thus, "Tambourines"
is, in essence, a morality play that makes a
thoughtful comment about the image of the preacher in the urban setting of the black experience
in the United States. And that image abounds in
Christian theology, even if it is slightly modified for a people to whom the song and the "holy
dance" foster the essence of religiousity, even
when they seem, to the unfeeling eye, pagan. The
greatest sin is consorting with absolute evil,
which is not Buddy Lomax per se. It is Buddy
Lomax motivated, sustained, and taught by Marty.
That evil transcends geography and time, but its
particularization--its "mask"--in the always
potentially destitute human condition of the
black American stands in boldest relief when it
is Marty-owned Buddy Lomax. With its eradica-
tion, so far as the church is concerned, the re-
deemable evil that mesmerizes Laura's side of the
preacher, falls away and Laura and Essie become
one.

"Rock Church"

    Elder William Jones, the central character in
"Rock Church," possessed no redeeming features.
He was "one of them rock-church preachers who
know how to make the spirit rise and the soul get
right," as Hughes introduces him to the reader.
Sometimes in the pulpit he would start talking
real slow, and his sermon would seem headed nowhere; but by the time he had finished preaching,
the walls of the building would be almost rent,
the doors busted open, and the benches turned
over from pure shouting. Jones was a great
preacher, but he was not satisfied with himself.
He wanted to be another Billy Graham or an Aimee
McPherson or a resurrected Reverend Becton. And
this over-riding ambition brought his downfall.

138

Ambition, alone, is no sin; but it is a dangerous motivation for a preacher. Especially for
one who had been for nearly a year pastor of one
of those little churches in the back alleys of
St. Louis that stayed open every night in the
week for preaching, singing, and praying, where
sisters came to shake tambourines, shout, sing
gospel songs, and get happy while the Reverend
preached the Word.

His format inspired confidence and religious
fervor. It made studied use of the erotic suggestions in the lyrics and the rhythm of the
songs the congregation sang every night in the
week. Jones opened and closed his part of the
service with the same song, "In His Hands." It
was one of those simple black religious songs:

In His hands!
In His hands!
I'm safe and sound
Settin' in Jesus' hand!

Jones' strutting rhythm led the congregation
toward the collection table every night while the
frenzy was upon them. Many, no doubt, sang and
imagined the "his" they sang about. They were,
they dreamed, in Jones' hands. And he tantalized
them with, "Come one! Come all! Come, my lambs
and put it down for Jesus," as the piano tingled
and the tambourines flew and the people shouted.

He did well, but St. Louis was not Chicago,
Detroit, or Harlem. He never thought of how his
church could serve the people who came to it now.
Instead, he thought always of how he could get
everybody talking about his church, and to get
the streets outside crowded and his name known
even to the far reaches of the nation.

But how? Everyone he knew who had achieved
anything like what he wanted from preaching had
used a special technique to lead to fame and
fortune. Billy Sunday had his sawdust trail;

139

Reverend Becton had two valets in the pulpit with
him as he cast off garment after garment in the
heat of preaching and he used up dozens of white
handkerchiefs every evening wiping his brow while
he preached. Aimee McPherson kept married and
divorced and made the front pages of newspapers
all over the country. Each of these gimmicks
had worked well. "I got to be news, too, in my
day and time," he fretted. "This town's too
small for me. I want the world to hear my name!"
He has some important characteristics of a preacher. He is a good preacher, and good-looking; his
cry was loud and his moan real deep. Some said
he moved the sisters in the congregation as they
had never been moved before. Hughes never shares
with the reader any language of Jones' sermons,
but one gets the impression that the moans and
cries are more histrionic than poetic. The sermons were part of the sensuality. In his youth,
before he had been converted, Jones had done a
little hustling around Vicksburg. He knew how to
appeal to women. Perhaps that skill could help
him achieve national renown.

The "lamb" Jones chose for his personal affection was Sister Maggie Bradford. She was far from
pretty; but she was well-fed, fat, good-natured,
brownskin, and prosperous. She owned four two-
family houses that she rented out, upstairs and
down. Her property, together with her sweet personality and her special interest in pleasing the
preacher, earned the unique status she enjoyed in
the church. Jones felt comfortable sharing his
deepest thoughts with her. Their mutual trust
led to the central incident of the short story:

>Elder Jones confided his personal am-
>bitions to said Sister Bradford one morning
>when he woke up to find her by his side.

>"I want to branch out Maggie," he said.
>"I want to be a really big man! Now, what
>can I do to get the 'tention of the world on
>me? I mean in a religious way?"

They thought and they thought. Since
it was a Fourth of July morning, and Sister
Maggie didn't have to go to collect rent,
they just lay there and thought.

Finally, Sister Maggie said, "Bill Jones,
you know something I ain't never forgot what
I seen as a child? There was a preacher down
in Mississippi named old man Eubanks who one
time got himself dead and buried and then rose
from the dead. Now, I ain't never forgot
that. Neither has nobody else in that part
of the Delta. That's something mem'rable.
Why don't you do something like that?"

Sister Maggie did not know how old man Eubanks
did it, because he never told anybody that. He
said it was the Grace of God. "It might a-been,"
Elder Jones agreed. But he was going to do something better than that. "I'm gonna be nailed on
a cross," he announced, and Sister Maggie exclaimed, "Do Jesus! Jones, you's a mess!"

She approved. But the preacher needed other
hands in order to pull off his miracle, so he
chose his head deacon, Brother Hicks, as a con-
federate. No one had bothered to tell the fairly
new minister that Brother Hicks had veen the favorite boyfriend of Sister Bradford before Elder
Jones arrived on the scene, and that the pillar
of the church--and now possessor of the preacher's plan for national recognition--still smoul-
dered over having been rejected in favor of the
Elder. "Hicks," he whispered to "Bulldog" Hicks,
"that miracle will make me the greatest minister
in the world. No doubt about it! Whan I get to
be world-renowned, Bulldog, and go traveling about
the firmament, I'll take you with me as my chief
deacon. You will be my right hand, and Sister
Maggie Bradford shall be my left hand." Bulldog
answered, "I hear you. I hope it comes true."
It will come true, Jones assured him, and he explained the plan in detail:

141

You know and I know that I ain't really
gonna die. Neither is I really gonna be
nailed. That's why I wants you to help me.
I wants you to have me a great big cross
made, higher than the altar--so high I has
to have a stepladder to get up to it to be
nailed thereon, and you to nail me. The
higher the better, so's they won't see the
straps. Now here you come and do the nailin'--nobody else but you. Put them nails
between my fingers and toes, not through
'em--between--and don't nail too deep. Leave
the heads kinder stickin' out. You get the
jibe? . . . . Then you and me'll stay right
on there in the church all night and day till
the next night when the people come back to
see me rise. Ever so often, you can let me
down to rest a little bit. But as long as
I'm on the cross, I play off like I'm dead,
particularly when reporters come around. On
Monday night--Halleujah! I will rise, and
take up the collection!

Such an announcement could hardly fail to attract an unusually large audience to Elder Jones'
church. Some doubted that he would be crucified,
stay dead, and rise. Sorrowing sisters of the
church cried even before the services began, but
their tears flowed even more freely as the new
cross, straight from the sawmill, loomed up behind the pulpit, decorated with big paper lilies
Sister Bradford had made. The Elder preached his
most powerful sermon and he announced in person
that he would be nailed to the cross and let the
breath pass from his body. But after twenty-four
hours, all the City of St. Louis "can be saved--
if they will just come out to see me."

There on the brink of greatness--at least in
his own world which he had already felt was too
little for his bigness--Elder jones reached his
moment of glory. But it was short-lived; for
Bulldog Hicks was not favorably impressed with
the histrionics gripping the church and the street

142

outside. He saw his chance to get even with
Jones. As the story tells it: "The old green
snake of jealousy began to coil around his heart,
right there in the meeting, right there on the
steps of the cross, at the very high point of the
ceremonies." "While I am nailin', I might as well
nail him right," Hicks thought. "A low-down
klinker--comin' here out of Mississippi to take
my woman away from me! He'll never know the
pleasure of my help in one o' his schemes to out-
divine Father! No, Sir!" And he hammered the
nails, not into the straps as he had been in-
structed, but into the flesh of the preacher--
just as cruelly as those men long ago had nailed
Jesus to the cross. As the Elder screamed in
pain and sought to escape the blows of Bulldog
Hick's hammer, the audience moaned and screamed,
with Sister Bradford leading the lot.

As the Reverend hissed, "Bulldog, I say, go
easy, this ain't real," Hicks turned his hammer
to the right side and kept up the hammering until
the Elder howled with pain. But the church was
moaning so loud with him that the members did not
realize the plan had gone awry. They did not
hear the bitter argument going on between the
preacher and the deacon. "I'll teach you happy-
headed jack-leg ministers to come to St. Louis
and think you all can walk away with any woman
you's a mind to," Hicks spat. "I'm gonna teach
you to leave my women alone. Here--here's a
nail!" As he aimed a great big spike at the palm
of Reverend Jones' left hand, the frightened
preacher let out a scream that could be heard two
blocks away. And he began to struggle to get
down, but the straps held him fast. When he
yelled a second blood-letting scream, the congregation suddenly became quiet. Everybody knew
no dying man could yell like that. When Sister
Bradford realized something had gone wrong, she
began to chant the song her pastor had told her
to start at the right moment. Even though the
nailing was not fully completed, she sang:

143

Elder Jones will rise again,
Elder Jones will rise again,
Rise again, rise again!
Elder Jones will rise again,
Yes, my lord!

But nobody joined her in song, so her voice
simply died out. Jones' voice could be heard
clearly now throughout the church as he called
Hicks names which were inappropriate for the
church, and certainly from one who was hanging
on the cross. Then he let out another frightful
scream and called, "Sister Maggie Bradford, lemme
down from here! Come and get me down . . . from
here!" As the deacon raised his hammer to strike
one more blow, everybody heard Jones dare him to
nail another nail and threaten to kill him stone-
dead with a forty-four if he did. "Just lemme
get loose from here, and I'll fight you like a
natural man," he gasped, twisting and turning
like a tree in a storm. As he called once more
for Sister Bradford to come and get him down, she
was utterly confused. What could possibly have
gone wrong so that the pastor would be calling
on her in public in the very midst of the thing
that was to bring him "famous-glory and make them
all rich preaching throughout the land with her
at his side?" "Elder Jones, you means you really
wants to get down?" she called from the Amen Corner. "Yes," said the Elder, "can't you hear? I
done called on you twenty times to let me down!"
When Hicks started to hammer yet another nail into her pastor, Sister Bradford leaped from her
seat, placing her ample weight against Deacon
Hicks, and with one foot sent him sprawling
across the pulpit. "You'll never crucify my
Elder," she cried, "not for real." She hastily
cut the straps from the Reverend's hands and feet
and let him slide to the floor, although his
feet were too bloody and sore for him to stand
without help. The church was deadly silent as
the preacher hobbled away with Sister Bradford's
help, cursing Deacon Hicks. "Stand back, Bulldog," Sister Maggie said to the deacon, "and let

144

him pass." Hicks stood back, the crowd murmured, and the preacher made his exit. He never did pastor in St. Louis again, neither did he fight Hicks. He just left town quietly.

Elder Jones possesses no redeeming feature, and the story contains little more than Jones. It is a burlesque of the image of the preacher in the storefront urban church who uses his physical attributes for his gratification. On its own terms, though, the tale implies an approval of Deacon Hicks and Sister Bradford which it denies to Elder Jones. They are not ministers of the Gospel; they are not actually exploiting people who believe in them, even when to do so is to engage in the ludicrous. They have a right to a love affair and Jones is not actually censored for his affair with Maggie Bradford. His ruthless over-riding ambition led him to plan and attempt to carry out a scheme that would have made him famous, in the unlikely event that it had been successful. But the sharpness of the implicit criticism and the satisfaction of Jones' downfall lies in his cruel mimic of one of the most sacred icons of the Christian religion--the Crucifixion. Yet, the idea was not actually original--that is the idea of mocking chauvinism on the part of the preacher. After all, Maggie Bradford, herself, had whetted Jones' imagination by telling him about the Reverend Eubanks who had risen from the dead. Moreover, the theatrics of Reverend Becton and Aimee Semple McPherson had attracted his imagination. It is an unpleasant story, which may very well represent bad taste to many readers, but it is consistent with Hughes' disdain for the preacher who expropriates religious devotion and money in the name of the church.

> "Gawd ain no lie! He ain no
>   lie!"
>
> --"Fire and Cloud"

Richard Wright (1908-1960) lived in Mississippi,
Arkansas, and Tennessee until he reached his
mid-teens. For the next ten years, he lived in
Chicago where he developed his skill in writing
poetry and prose fiction. He left Chicago for
New York City where he lived for the next several years. He spent the rest of his life in
Europe, making his home in Paris, France, and
traveling in many parts of the world. His best
known fiction works include two collections of
short stories. Uncle Tom's Children (1938) and
Eight Men (1961); and the novels, Native Son
(1940); Black Boy (1945); The Outsider (1953);
The Long Dream (1958); Lawd, Today (1963); and
Savage Holiday (   ). "Fire and Cloud," one
of the short stories included in Uncle Tom's
Children and Native Son provide images of the
preacher for this study that are taken from
Richard Wright's fiction.

RICHARD WRIGHT: PRIESTS AND POTENCY

   Publication of Richard Wright's Uncle Tom's
Children marked a milestone in the promising
young writer's professional career. One of the
four novellas, "Fire and Cloud," had won the
$500 first prize in a Story Magazine contest and
had attracted the attention of literary critics
in the United States and abroad. Richard Wright
became not merely a prize winner but a new Amer-

147

ican wtiter. Some reviewers called him the
voice of a new generation of black America--
a new direction from the Harlem Renaissance
writers--one whose voice was hard but reminis-
cent of the melody of the old spirituals. The
four pieces of prose fiction in the new publication generated conflict among black literary
figures. Sterling Brown thought the stories
weak because of excessive use of coincidence,
poor structure, and limpid characterization.
Zora Neale Hurston, who considered herself the
leading black fiction writer of the time and
whose Their Eyes Were Watching God had been
criticized by Wright for its failure to seek new
directions for the black writer in America,
criticized the stories for the unauthentic dialect and their slavish adherence to the Communist Party line. Alain Locke, the dean of Afro-
American letters, predicted a major literary
career for Wright because he had demonstrated
that he could use the novella to carry the
strength of the epic tragedy that was the black
experience in the United States.

Locke was correct in predicting a major literary career for Wright, and he appropriately
analyzed the use of the novella as a tour de
force for the vitality of the black American experience. Wright explained that "Fire and Cloud"
was designed to show the development of political awareness among Negroes. Inasmuch as the
preacher is the acknowledged leader among black
Americans, he often faced a crisis of conscience.
That particular focus on existential elements
was not new in Afro-American letters, but how
does a writer handle volatile elements of conventional Christianity, as practiced by blacks,
with a divinely impatient black man whose social
consciousness emblazons upon him the need for a
new definition of race leadership? Specifically, how does that man as preacher learn Wright's
truth that there is no such thing as an unpoli-
tical man; that only the most passive of men can
sit and see themselves destroyed without fight-

ing back with resources that are at least potentially efficient for the struggle he faces?
To Wright, a preacher who finds himself in this
uncomfortable but inevitable crisis, enlarges
his sights beyond the conventional care of his
congregation. Such an image of the preacher is
a legitimate symbol of black power that would
lie dormant without the preacher as the catalyst
for releasing its social energy.

Experience outside his home taught Wright
what he called the social crime America per-
pretrated upon the black masses. Inside his
family, he learned to rebel against the strict
religious practices his grandmother imposed upon
her household when he lived there. The responsibility of the individual, as it had been ex-
pounded in the early 20th century by Booker T.
Washington, in particular, is totally rejected
by Wright's social vision in each of the stories
in Uncle Tom's Children. For the natural pro-
gression of the education of the race from tragic individualism toward corporate strength of
the people becomes one of the author's major
racial statements. Religion is always futile to
Wright; that is, religion as it is practiced
conventionally by the black church. But the
church does contain a ready-made community organization that, with the proper leadership and
progressive orientation to its potential strength
as it joins hands with other institutions
similarly situated, can realize society's highest hope. The millenium cannot come outside the
collected memory of the race, and it will use
the poetry and the music of the race's best in-
stitution--the church. It is the writer's responsibility to dramatize this truth.

Between "Fire and Cloud" and Native Son,
Wright's image of the preacher moves from celebration of the community-conscious, pragmatic
leader who painfully sacrifices personal commitment to his immediate family for the larger
good to the totally incompetent preacher whose

rhetoric and accoutrements of religion cannot
help the person he wishes most to bring solace.
More importantly, even in his impotence, that
preacher uses his only fire to condemn Communism,
declaring that people who stir up trouble should
be avoided. This stark contrast between these
two works represents an essence of Wright's social vision.

"Fire and Cloud"

     Dan Taylor experiences in the closing para-
graph of "Fire and Cloud" a "baptism of clean joy"
as he leads a demonstration sharply similar to
the civil rights marches which were to come twenty years into the future, as the Southern, small
town Baptist preacher takes on heroic stature
in a communal role that has been thrust upon him,
and arouses and sustains within him sufficient
strength and intelligence and leadership needed
in that time and place. Within the pattern of
an allegory of good and evil, the author moves
from polemicist to contemporary myth-maker,
blending skillfully and credibly the argument
that "freedom belongs to the strong"; that the
economic basis on which men are strong or weak
transcends race and religion; that the new day
in the United States required a joining of
forces that share poverty to march against those
who withhold from them the creature comforts
of life; that such a strength of spirit gives
form and substance to an enrichment of the meaning of religion; that that new meaning becomes
the hallmark of the appropriate leadership role
which the black preacher must perform in and for
his community. Taylor in the final lines of
the story, marches in the "sea of black and
white faces," hardly realizing the superficial
differences of their color, or their church af-
filiation. The whites are not members of his
congregation; they remain clear of the petty
bickering among Taylor's deacons. The park that
marks the point at which the whites will join
the march still represents a visible and physi-

cal separation of the races which the author accepts. It is the cause, though, which brings the town's poor--black and white--into the sea of faces. Clearly, Dan Taylor is the leader; for it is he whom the Mayor calls to tell, ". . . they can get food if they go back home, peacefully." It is he, too, who in his new strength and release from the shame which his impotence as nominal leader had imposed upon him throughout all of his life, steps outside his exaggeratedly humble role and cries back, "Yuh tell 'em, yu Honah!"

The story gets told through Dan Taylor's experiences, and it is also through him that the image of the preacher is projected. "Fire and Cloud" explores a social thesis. The character of the preacher almost single-handedly leads the community to a solution to their problem and, at the same time, provides the equally important lesson to the young which Dan Taylor teaches his son. As parent and preacher, his role is a double entendre, proving that the measure of a man in what he can tell his son, and that the measure of preacher lies in his power to demonstrate "Gawd ain't no lie!" As Taylor experiences the story's apotheosis, his eyes grow dim with tears, and in his blurred vision he sees the sky tremble, the buildings wavering as if about to topple, and the earth shakes. The Lord is cleaning up "this ol worl" and making a new Heaven and a New Earth, as Dan had always known He would someday. He had known it because in his vision he sees it taking place before his eyes. His exhultation with the and larger congregation of the poor comes through as he mumbles aloud the social truth this experience has taught him: "Freedom belongs to the strong!" But the reality has come through his sagacity in handling his community problem and through his role as preacher.

A hint of the "tear and the smile" surrounds the Reverend Dan Taylor as he is introduced into the story, walking alone, mopping his brow and

reciting to himself the ancient rime, so well-
known to the black experience:

A naught's a naught
N five's a figger
All for the white man
None for the nigger.

Rime-making and reality rush in upon his consciousness as his shoulders shake in half-laugh,
half-shudder and he surveys the visible essence
of the difference between the dim buildings of
the town lying sprawling mistily on the crest of
a far hill and the cluster of black huts where he
and his own people live. "Seems like the white
folk jus erbout owns this whole worl'!", he thinks
bitterly. "We black folks is jus los in one big
white fog." But the symbolic essence of his actual and potential link between the black and
white worlds of his town, he flexes his lips slowly and speaks under his breath the glimmer of
hope he believes lives:

They could do something. They could do
something, awright! Mebbe if five uh
six of us marched downtown we could scare
em inter doin something! Lord knows, mebbe
them Reds is right.

Potential solution? Yes, and it had already
been suggested, even urged by the Reds. But Dan
Taylor, true to the conventional image of the
black leader, wanted to agree with the Reds only
as a last resort. He knew by sight and sound
every black man, woman, and child who lived in
his community. How could he tell them that the
white woman downtown had said in her dry metallic
voice: "I'm sorry, Taylor. You'll have to do
the best you can. Explain it to them, make them
understand that we can't do anything. Everybody's hungry, and after all, its no harder on
your people than it is on ours. Tell them they'll
just have to wait."

Her words did not solve Dan's problem, but they did motivate his thinking. That white woman who handed out the dollars did not know anything about being hungry, he thought. As he walked back closer to his community, he agonized over his apparent impotence to lead and help his people. He was "a man called by Gawd to preach" and yet he had no answers to the hungry people who looked to him for leadership. Maybe the Communists were right. There was plenty of food in the fields around him, but his folks were still hungry. This incongruity caused him to sermonize to himself briefly, as he fused economics and religion once more, saying to the countryside:

The good Lawd's gonna clean up this ol worl some day! He's gonna make a new Heaven n a new Earth! He's gonna do it in a eye-twinklin change! He's gonna do it! Things cant go on like this forever. God knows they cant!

Fortified with his own assurance, and indicating to the reader that his faith in his religion brought that assurance, Taylor decided he had no choice but to return to his people and tell them what he has been told. He has gone to Olympus and the voice of the gods of society had told him everybody was having a hard time. His people would simply have to wait. Taking the message back was simple enough, but it could hardly still the distress within his own heart. He had earned his right to the bounty of the land; further, he understood the call to preach and to save the black people by preaching the gospel and guiding his people:

This was the land on which the Great God Almighty had first let him see the light of His blessed day. This was the land on which he had first taken unto himself a wife, leaving his mother and father to cleave to her. And it was on the green slopes of these struggling hills that his

first-born son, Jimmy, had romped and
played, growing to a strong, upright
manhood. He wagged his head, musing:
Lawd, them wuz the good ol days. . . .
There had been plenty to eat; the blessings
of God had been overflowing. He had toiled
from sunup to sundown, and in the cool of
the evening his wife, May, had taught him
to read and write. Then God had spoken to
him, a quiet, deep voice coming out of the
black night; God had called him to preach
His word, to spread it to the four corners
of the earth, to save His black people.
And he had obeyed God and had built a church
on a rock which the very gates of Hell
could not prevail against. Yes, he had been
like Moses, leading his people out of the
wilderness into the Promised Land. He
sighed, walking and taking his coat from
his left arm and tucking it under his right.
Yes, things had been clear-cut then. In
those days there had stretched before his
eyes a straight and narrow path and he had
walked in it, with the help of a Gracious
God. On Sundays he had preached God's Word,
and on Mondays and Tuesdays and Wednesdays
and Thursdays and Fridays and Saturdays he
had taken old Bess, his mule, and his plow
and he had broke God's ground. For a moment while walking through the dust and remembering his hopes of those early years
he seemed to feel again the plow trembling
in his calloused hands and hear the earth
cracking and breaking open, black, rich
and damp; it seemed he could see old Bess
straining forward with the plow, swishing
her tail and tossing her head and snorting
now and then. Yes, there had been something
in those good old days when he had walked
behind his plow, between the broad green
earth and a blue sweep of sunlit sky; there
had been in it all a surge of will, clean,
full, joyful; the earth was his and he was
the earth's; they were one; and it was that

joy and will and oneness in him that God
had spoken to when He had called him to
preach His Word, to save His black people,
to lead them, to guide them, to be a shep-
herd to His flock. But now the whole thing
was giving way, crumbling in his hands,
right before his eyes. And every time he
tried to think of some way to stop it, he
saw wide grey eyes behind icily white spec-
tacles. He mopped his brow again. Mabbe
Hadley n Green's right. . . . Lawd, Ah don
know what t do! Ef Ah fight fer things
the white folk say Ahma bad nigger stirrin
up trouble. N ef Ah don do nothin, we
starve. . . . But somethings gotta be done!
Mabbe ef we hada demonstration like Hadley
n Green said, we could scare them white
folks inter doin something. . . .

   He looked at the fields again, half-
wistfully, half-curiously. Lawd, we could
make them ol fiels bloom ergin. We could
make em feed us. Thas whut Gawd put em
there fer. Plows could break and hoes
could chop and hands could pick and arms
could carry. . . . On and on that could
happen and people could eat and feel as he
had felt with the plow handles trembling
in his hands, following old Bess, hearing
the earth cracking and breaking because he
willed it, because the earth was his. And
they could sing as he had sung when he and
May were first married; sing about picking
cotton, fishing, hunting, about sun and
rain. They could. . . . But whuts the usa
thinkin erbout stuff like this? Its all
gone now. . . . And he had to go and tell
his congregation, the folks the Great God
Almighty had called him to lead to the
Promised Land--he had to tell them that the
relief would give them no food.

Wright does not explain the specifics of the
lfare Department's failure to provide food to

Taylor's people, but it does become clear that food is available. The problem is stated too simply, but the full green fields about him and the hunger of his people motivate Dan Taylor's thought and action. The power structure of the town, though, does not present Dan's only antagonism. Deacon Smith, with his scheming and plotting, was ever ready to run and tell the white folks something the preacher did wrong or whisper about him behind his back, or take his congregation away from him. Feeling akin to Jesus when he was being tempted by the Devil, Taylor thought of Deacon Smith as "a black snake in the grass," and decided to preach about Jesus' temptation next Sunday.

Approaching his home in his aloneness, the preacher's son ran to tell him the Mayor and the Chief of Police were waiting for him in his parlor. The town said there would be a demonstration and Deacon Smith had told the congregation Taylor was mixed up with the Reds. So the town's power structure waited for the preacher in his parlor and his deacons waited in the Bible Room. "Good Lawd, whut a mess!" Taylor said of his predicament.

He opened the door of his church upon a crescendo of voices. The committee that had been sent to call upon the Mayor had returned. They said they had been run out of the Mayor's office and the police had been turned on them. Men and women surrounded the preacher, crying for help for their hungry children. What are we going to do? they ask him from all sides. His helplessness shamed him. Taylor turned into his role as conventional preacher at this moment and asked his congregation to join in prayer, more to quiet them than in expectation of miraculous help. The room grew still as he prayed to the God who made the sun, moon, stars, seas, and mankind, and the beasts of the field; to the God who, strong and powerful, ruled the world; He who brought the children of Israel out of Egypt

156

and made the dry bones rise out of the valley
and lived and saved the Hebrew children from the
fiery furnace. Then, specifying his invocation,
he prayed:

The white folks say we cant raise nothin on
Yo earth! They done put the lans of the
worl in their pockets! They done fenced em
off n nailed em down! Theys a-tryin t take
Yo place, Lawd!
Yuh put us in this worl n said we could live
in it! Yuh said this worl wuz Yo own! Now
show us the sign like yuh showed Saul! Show
us the sign n we'll ack! We ast this in the
name of Yo son Jesus who died tha we might
live! Amen!

Still, his congregation pressed for concrete
answers. "Can't yuh do somethin?" one woman
asked, indicating the insufficiency of prayer and
the role of the preacher-poet in the necessity.
His wife joined in the chorus of questions, and
Taylor told her she had to lie for him, explaining, "What kin we do but lie?" He wanted his
wife to tell the Mayor he is sick in bed but is
getting dressed to come to talk to him and to
tell the deacons he is talking with the Mayor.
At the same time he asked Hadley and Green to
come to find a solution. He learned from the
Communists that the success of the demonstration
the next day would depend on him. "Ah done told
you Ah cant let them whites know Ahm calling
folks to demonstrate," the preacher complained.

All factions of the community were helpless
without Taylor's cooperation. He needed only to
lend his name to get a crowd to participate in
the demonstration, but the preacher felt he had
no right to send his people into the streets to
be attacked by the police. Moreover, a failure
now would nullify any chances he may have to help
his people in the future. Hadley chided Taylor,
"If you made it known you would fight rather than
ask, the power structure would dislike you, yes,

157

but it would make the officials give something
to all black people--not just you." That attack
is unfair. Taylor was not asking for anything
for himself, but he knew full well only he could
affect a coalition of poor whites and blacks.
Yet, he maintained he would act only as God directed him. As he passed through the dim-light-
ed sanctuary of his church to talk to the Chief
and the Mayor, Taylor lifted his eyes to the
figure of Christ on a huge snow-white cross and
prayed, "God, help me to say and do the right
thing."

The Mayor began the conference with, "This is
Dan, Chief, the boy I was telling you about."
To Dan's, "How yuh, Mister Chief?" Chief Bolton
grunted, "Hello, boy," adding deeper insult to
the injury Dan already felt. The Mayor summed
up his reasons for coming to the church. Dan,
he said, is the "only nigger" he would come and
talk to because he has known him for 25 years
and has faith in him. He has helped black people
in the past, especially in saving Scott from a
lynching, and can help them again. Dan simply
must keep his people from marching with the Reds
who are bent on trying to wreck the country. The
Chief of Police and the Mayor warned Dan sternly
and appealed to him for help. His crisis was
clear. Taylor listened attentively. When the
threatening was over, he repeated what he had
said many times: his people were hungry; they
were marching because they did not know what
else to do. "What do they think they're goin to
get by marchin?" the Chief thundered, and Taylor
replied they think they will get bread. "It
wont get them a Goddam crumb," Chief Bolton
promised. The Mayor continued to placate Dan to
extract from him a pledge to keep the peace
among the town's black poor. Taylor decides to
march if his church will. "Them white folks
can't kill us all," he reasoned, when he told
his congregation about his conversation with the
Mayor. He would march with his people.

The gruesome incident of Dan Taylor's abduction and beating by a mob of white men on the night before the demonstration does not give added reason for the preacher's decision. He had already decided to march despite the threat and warnings because he believed sincerely that the action would demonstrate solidarity among black and white persons who shared poverty. He had rejected the concept of "safe leadership" and was motivated to exercise a more acceptable concept of self-hood. He had absolutely no sympathy with Communist politics, but Hadley and Green had at least offered help and support while the town's officials provided humiliation and threats and continued hunger. A sincerely religious man such as Dan would be repulsed by the bad taste of his tormentors who made him pray while they were beating him. Interestingly, he prayed the Lord's Prayer, not the prayer he used with his congregation. And even as he prayed "the white man's prayer," the leader of the mob continued to lash him. Only then did his own raw hate rise to meet the mob as he screamed out, "Awright, kill me! Tie me n kill me! Yuh white trash cowards, kill me! We'll git yuh white trash some day! So help me, Gawd, we'll git you!" This reaction is his "baptism into reality."

As he struggled back to his community, late at night after his flogging, Dan experienced a completely understandable reaction to Christianity as he recognized the steeple of the white church whose preacher he knew. "Spose Ah go to Houston?" he asked himself, and answered that even though the two men preached the same gospel, the white minister would not take him in and help him. "Some day theys gonna burn in Gawd Almighty's fire," he assured himself repeatedly as he moved through the white neighborhood. The real worth of the beating scene lies in Dan's relationship to his son, Jimmy, when he returned home:

"Whuts the mattah, Pa? Yuh sick?"

159

"Close the do n set down, son!"

Taylor could hear Jimmy's breathing, then
a chair scraping over the floor and the
soft rustle of Jimmy's clothes as he sat.

"Whuts the mattah, Pa? Whut happened?"

Taylor stared in the darkness and slowly
licked his swollen lips. He wanted to
speak, but somehow could not. Then he
stiffened, hearing Jimmy rise.

"Set down, son!"

"But , Pa. . . ."

Fire seethed not only in Taylor's back, but
all over, inside and out. It was the fire
of shame. The questions that fell from
Jimmy's lips burned as much as the whip had.
There rose in him a memory of all the times
he had given advice, counsel, and guidance
to Jimmy. And he wanted to talk to him now
as he had in the past. But his impulses
were deadlocked. Then suddenly he heard
himself speaking, hoarsely, faintly. His
voice was like a whisper rising from his
whole body.

"They whipped me, son. . . ."

"Whipped yuh? Who?"

Jimmy ran to the bed and touched him.

"Son, set down!"

Taylor's voice was filled with a sort of
tense despair. He felt Jimmy's fingers
leaving him slowly. There was a silence
in which he could hear only his own breath
struggling in his throat.

160

"Yuh mean the white folks?"

Taylor buried his face in his pillow and
tried to still the heaving in his chest.

"They beat me, son. . . ."

"Ahll git a doctah!"

"Naw!"

But yuhs hurt!"

"Naw, lock the do! Don let May in
here. . . ."

"Godamm them white bastards!"

"Set down, son!"

"Who wuz they, Pa?"

"Yuh cant do nothin, son. Yuhll have t
wait. . . ."

"Wes been waitin too long! All we do is
wait, wait!"

Jimmy's footsteps scuffed across the floor.
Taylor sat up.

"Son?"

"Ahma git mah gun n git Pete n Bob n Joe n
Sam! Theyll see they cant do this t us!"

Dan has learned best, "yuh cant do nothin erlone," as he tells this truth to his son. Also,
he learned that his church has voted to dismiss
him as pastor, suggesting an incredible swift-
ness in the plot. But this news led to Dan's
sincere and futile utterance which best typifies
his dilemma throughout the plot of the novella.
He complained that it seems like God has left

161

him alone; he exclaimed that he would die for his people if he only knew how; he castigated himself for what seemed to him like living on his knees all his life, begging and pleading with the white folks to help his people, only to be kicked by them; that what they were pressuring him to do now was to give them his soul; that the greatest indignity he suffered was that if he so much as talked like a man, they tried to kill him.

This tragic insight--what it means to be a black preacher in America in a setting such as his town--strengthened his resolve. Now, instead of holding his son, the embodiment of the younger generation back, he teaches him. Now a man can tell his son, "It's the people we mus gid wid us! Wes empty n weak this way! The reason we cant do nothin is cause wes so much erlone!"

Dan Taylor now has found a new religion, but it is built solidly upon the old one. In terms of the values of the story, it is proletarian. As a thesis story, the central character learns a religion that is stronger than that he had already practiced sincerely. It is religion for living; as he tells his son, it is still letting God be so real in your life that everything you do is because of him, only there is a difference now:

> . . . . Its the people! Theys the ones whut mus be real t us! Gawds wid the people! N the peoples gotta be real as Gawd t us! We cant hep ourselves er the people when wes erlone. Ah been wrong erbout a lotta things Ah tol yuh, son. Ah tol yuh them things cause Ah thought they wuz right. Ah tol yuh t work hard n climb t the top. Ah tol yuh folks would lissen t yuh then. But they wont, son! All the will, all the strength, all the power, all the numbahs is in the people!

162

Yuh cant live by yoself! When they beat
me tonight, they beat me. . . . There
wuznt nothin Ah could do but lay there n
hate n pray n cry. . . . Ah couldnt <u>feel</u>
mah people, Ah couldnt <u>see</u> mah people,
Ah couldnt <u>hear</u> mah people. . . . All Ah
could feel <u>wuz</u> tha whip cuttin mah blood
out. . . .

The beating has been a purgation for him in
that it has taken a potentially effective black
leader and made him actually effective. His
doubts have been consumed by the fire the whip
of his attackers heaped upon his body. Accomma-
dation of any kind gives way to confrontation,
but a new organization is not necessary. The
old one only needs new direction and vitality.
The old leader only needs a more concrete and
more comprehensive view of his leadership responsibilities and potentialities. The Reds
did not need to convert Dan Taylor to Communism.
The power structure of the town taught him the
lesson Hadley and Green most wanted him to learn.
They consolidated the elements of effective
leadership so that the religious blacks and the
hungry blacks and whites and the Red organizers
and the city power structure could combine into
a federation which had at first seemed totally
impossible.

The new organism sprang forth fully grown
when the group of marchers on the first day returned from the town. They assembled in the
church's waiting room with arms in slings; necks
wrapped in white cloths; legs bound in blood-
stained rags. "Look at what yuh done done,"
deacon Smith cried out to Taylor, whose eyes
went from face to face. He knew them all. Every
Sunday they sat in the pews of his church, praying, singing, and trusting in the God he preached to them. They were lonely and he wanted to
break down that loneliness, but he did not know
how. Conventional singing and praying and trusting had isolated them; they were joined in their

own misery. But no parable from the Bible sprang
to Dan's lips now; for none spoke to the meaning
of the human condition they all faced. So the
preacher stood naked and alone. His religion--
and theirs-- needed a dimension which passed
their present understanding. When his people now
asked him what they should do; when they said,
"the white folks can do no more than theys already done"; when someone reported the poor
whites would meet the poor blacks at the park,
the march was on. When Dan told the congregation about his beating; that they made him take
the name of Gawd in vain; that as he struggled
back home that morning he had seen a sign; the
one-ness became known. He told them they must
get together; that their life is suffering and
fire and hell; that no one could bear that fire
alone. "We'll go if you go," the crowd cried out
in reply. They sang as they marched, and the
"cloud and the fire" they sang about represented
the new direction and dimension to their religion. Others joined them along the way, and the
whites came out to meet them at the park--the
poor whites who, because they were hungry, poured
out into the streets to join in the black procession to meet the power structure. Dan felt
himself moving between the silent lines of policemen and told himself no one would bother
such a demonstration of solidarity:

> They were tramping on pavement now. And
> the blue-coated men stood still and silent.
> Taylor saw Deacon Smith standing on the
> curb, and Smith's face merged with the
> faces of the others, meaningless, lost.
> Ahead was the City Hall, white and clean
> in the sunshine. The autos stopped at
> the street corners while the crowd passed;
> and as they entered the downtown section
> people massed quietly on the sidewalks.
> Then the crowd began to slow, barely moving.
> Taylor looked ahead and wondered what was
> about to happen; he wondered without fear;
> as though whatever would or could happen

164

could not hurt this many-limbed, many-legged, many-handed crowd that was he.
He felt May clinging to his sleeve. Jimmy was peering ahead. A policeman came running up to him.

The comic inversion upon which the story turns and makes its main point occurs when the Mayor calls to Dan, "Tell your people not to make any trouble." The crisis was passed and the object won. The image of the preacher--never actually tarnished--emerges as a refreshing and refined blend of ancient sacrifice and contemporary leadership. Clearly a story intended to show the wisdom of the Communist approach to social problem solving, "Fire and Cloud" never deprecates the preacher. Because of the sense of the needs of the community and knowing the avenues to fulfillment of that need require a leadership which only the preacher can provide, the story makes him the sine qua non for that society. The strength of the proletariat does not necessarily lie in formal education or personal polish. Its leader needs, more than any one other quality, a sincere desire to properly lead his people. He needs new depths to his own religious experiences, as is indicated in the final march when Dan says to himself, aloud, "Gawd ain no lie! He ain no lie!"

As an allegory of good and of evil, "Fire and Cloud" excoriates the unapproved attitude of the white power structure in the town. All characters, with the exception of Deacon Smith, can find salvation within the story's unfolding ethic.

With the power of the strength of his own basic character and the forging of his resolve in the "fire" of his suffering, Dan Taylor reaches an essential apotheosis. And as much of the community as can receive salvation join him in the socially important ritual which ends the story. Mayor Bolton represents the official evil which

165

comes to recognize the essential good in Taylor and the other marchers, even if he does so under duress. He is teachable. Deacon Smith, though, is beyond redemption. He has personified absolute evil in a kind of villainy which honors no person or principle. He stands faceless in the crowd viewing but not participating in the "baptism of clean joy." He has envied and persecuted Dan Taylor with his cantankerous action in the congregation. His paramount evil lies in his duplicity. He has informed the white folks of the black folks' plans to march. Too, on the story's standards of morality, he is incapable of grasping the significance of the experience in which he has the opportunity to participate. He is the only person who is specifically excluded from the communion of those who demonstrate their new power and their knowledge. He is more reprehensible than the Mayor or the Chief of Police; for when Reality bursts upon them they recognize it.

Dan Taylor is not an "Uncle Tom." He has believed that the best interest of his people was served by his obsequiously pleading their case to the whites. But the careful reader and the person who fully understands the Dan Taylors of the world, fully understands some other dimensions in his image of himself. He hates the persons he must cater to in order to gain any advantage for his people; he repeatedly tells Hadley and Green that he is unwilling to send his people out to be beaten and perhaps killed by hostile policemen; he stands up to all the publics he is required to please--his wife and son, his church officers, his congregation, and the Mayor and Chief of Police, and the Communists--and firmly finds his own way to best serve his community and his people. As he expresses it, he depends on God to guide him. All the publics he has to please ridicule him, indirectly or directly, for this stubborn dependence upon his religion. Whether he uses it as

a ruse or not cannot be determined definitively;
but it is clear that he uses it steadfastly.

Wright might have intended to show once again
the futility of religion in social action. But
the sensitive reader has to enter into Dan Taylor's mind with the preacher throughout his ago-
nies in the plot of the story. What should he
do? What can he do? How can he show clearly
that he is the leader of his people, as he believes he is, and lead them to their advantage?
These are the questions which consume him. And
they represent, to a large extent, what may be
called "the theology of hope" which is far from
a non-Christian view, even if Wright had intended the story as a rejection of Dan Taylor's religion. For within the philosophy of hope in
theology, there is the possibility of the revo-
lutionary, the promise of brotherhood where there
is none, and the glory of the vision of the future. Despair, on the other hand, presumes a
non-fillment of the promise of that preacher's
view of religion. Accordingly, when he learns
there is something he and people can do--some-
thing to which all persons similarly situated
can subscribe--that same religion which he has
practiced all of his life causes him to realize
"Gawd ain no lie!" right alongside his realization that freedom belongs to the strong. This
total image of the preacher--one who respects
the majority of his people, who knows each of
them well, who seeks sincerely to serve his
people in what he believes is a manifestation of
God's will--is influenced to action only by the
method of the demonstration of solidarity which
the Reds suggest. They have not daunted his
fervor, nor have they managed him. They are no
more effective in using him as a tool than are
the Mayor and the Chief of Police. One may believe that in the end, Dan and the Reds are one,
but such a conclusion is presumptuous. Dan Taylor, the preacher, was the leader of his people
when the story opened and he is their leader at

the end, but his method of demonstrating the strength of his leadership has changed radically.

Native Son

Richard Wright endows Reverend Hammond, Bigger Thomas' mother's preacher, with no redeeming other sincerity. He is the stereotyped black preacher whose piety enslaves him to an image that can hardly serve the youthful rebel of his day who seeks to throw off the yokes of the negative effects of economic and religious serfdom. He is as guilty of condemning the creative and regenerative energies of black youth. as is the white philanthropist. He exploits his own people with his worthless religion even as the Daltons impoverish them with their spurious contributions to charities. Neither makes the level of commitment Wright demands of persons who hold in their hands the power to affect the quality of life of the masses of Americans. Neither enobles the community. Ironically, each family fails to understand his true relationship to the population Bigger Thomas and his family and associates represent. Hammond and Dalton are <u>blind</u> in the special way Wright uses that metaphor. <u>Native Son</u> does not unfold into a new social consciousness for either of them. They are representational characters rather than "rounded" ones. The novel is Bigger Thomas' story. Hammond and Dalton relate to him, however. Hammond is patterned by Wright to illustrate an image of the preacher that is radically different from Daniel Taylor of "Fire and Cloud."

Bigger Thomas had killed Mary Dalton and Bessie Mears by the time Reverend Hammond enters the novel. He smothered Mary during his first night as her father's chauffeur. She gets drunk with the young Communist, Jan Erlone, after Bigger has driven them to a Communist

168

cell meeting. He believes he should not leave
the girl outside the house in the car. It is
snowing and the Daltons would expect a servant
to take care of their daughter who they believe
has gone to a night class at a university. Bigger takes Mary to her room. She refuses to remain quiet, so he puts a pillow over her head to
silence her moaning. He is completely condi-
tioned to know that any white person who would
find him in a white girl's room would believe he
was there to try to rape her. He kills her accidentally when he hears Mrs. Dalton, who is
blind, coming into Mary's room. Her death comes
totally accidentally. After Bigger realizes she
is dead he tries in desperation to find a way to
dispose of her body and crams it into the furnace he has been employed to fire. Fear over-
whelms him, and he looks for a way to shift the
blame to anyone else. He knows Jan is a "Red."
Although he has no idea of what "Reds" are, he
knows the public does not like them. When he
becomes the chief suspect in the death of Mary,
Bigger comes to view his accidental act of killing her as the generation of a new personality.
He believes he has killed a representative of
that which he hates and fears most. Now he
feels he can compete with the white world. Perhaps he can even control it. He ensnares his
girl friend Bessie as an accomplice in his plot
to extract money from the "Reds" and he does
murder her when she impedes his flight from the
pursuing police. He is captured, surrounded and
overpowered by the white forces he hates and
fears. The entire city has focused on his
flight and apprehension. He has become for a
brief period a cause celebre.

Reverend Hammond enters the novel at a well-
calculated point. Bigger had fainted at the inquest, and when he recovered, a policeman came
into his cell and handed him an armful of newspapers with the comment, "Here you are, boy.
You're in 'em all." When the policeman left,
Bigger spread out the issues of the Tribune and

read a headline, NEGRO RAPIST FAINTS AT INQUEST.
The first paragraph of one news story read:

> Overwhelmed by the sight of his accusers,
> Bigger Thomas, Negro sex-slayer, fainted
> dramatically this morning at the inquest
> of Mary Dalton, millionaire Chicago heir-
> ess.

The long story, despite its inaccuracies,
brought Bigger to realize he was going to die
for the crime. His mind wandered off as if he
were trying to make a decision. He reviewed his
feelings the night he had gripped the icy edges
of the water tank while search lights and sirens
surrounded him and he had known his capture
would come any minute. He closed his eyes and
re-opened them abruptly to find the door of his
cell opening. When the door swung in, he saw a
black face. A tall, well-dressed black man came
forward and paused. Neither spoke for the moment, and Bigger raised up on his elbows from
his prone position on his cot. The man came
over to him and "stretched forth his dingy palm,
touching Bigger's hand."

"Mah po' boy! May the good Lawd have mercy
on yuh," he said, and remembered the man was his
mother's pastor. He had come at the very moment
Bigger was re-enacting the last details of his
flight from the police. The minister, without
knowing it, became to Bigger another kind or law
enforcement officer. No matter how kindly his
gestures nor how consoling his words might have
intended to be, his image was drawn on the screen
of Bigger's mind, and that is one of the ways in
which Wright presents the preacher to the reader.
From the moment Bigger recognizes him, he closes
his heart and tries to stifle all feeling inside
himself. He fears the preacher will make him
feel remorseful for the act that has given him
a sense of manhood and importance for the first
time in his life. Somehow, the preacher represented for Bigger the image he associated with

170

what he had just read about himself in the <u>Tri-</u>
<u>bune</u>.

This scene follows:

"How yuh feel, son?" the man asked; he
did not answer and the voice hurried on:
"Yo ma ast t' come 'n' see yuh. She wants
to come too."

The preacher knelt upon the concrete floor
and closed his eyes. Bigger clamped his
teeth and flexed his muscles; he knew what
was coming.

Lawd Jesus, turn Yo' eyes 'n' look inter
the heart of this po' sinner! Yuh said
mercy wuz always Yo's 'n' if we ast fer it
on bended knee Yuh'd po' it out inter our
hearts 'n' make our cups run over! We's
astin Yuh t' po' out Yo' mercy now, Lawd!
Po' it out fer this po' sinner boy who
stan's deep in need of it! Ef his sins be
scarlet, Lawd, wash 'em white as snow!
Fergive 'im fer whutever he's done, Lawd.
Let the light of Yo' love guide 'im th'u
these hard days! 'n' he'p them who's a-
tryin' to he'p 'im, Lawd. Enter inter
they hearts 'n' breathe compassion on they
sperits! We ast this in the nama Yo' Son
Jesus who died on the cross 'n' gave us
the mercy of Yo' love! Ahmen. . .

The preacher had gone into his conventional
role as sincere poet of the invocation of the
power of God into the personal affairs of his
congregation. This time the son of one of his
members. He plays his role unhesitatingly and
sincerely. It never occurred to him that Bigger
was totally rejecting what he represented. To
Bigger, the preacher's prayer was the old voice
of his mother, telling him about suffering, of
hope, of love beyond the world. And he loathed
it because it made him feel as condemned and

171

guilty as the voice of those who hated him, the author tells us. Still conscious of his duty to his congregation, the preacher moved further into his role as he saw it and understood it:

Son. . . fergit ever'thing but yo' soul,
son. Take yo' mind off ever'thing but
eternal life. Fergit whut the newspaper
say. Fergit yuh's black. Gawd looks past
yo' skin 'n' inter yo' soul, son. He's
lookin' at the only parta yuh that's His.
He wants yuh 'n' He loves yuh. Give yo'se'f
t' 'Im, son. Lissen, lemme tell yuh why
yuh's here; lemme tell yuh a story that'll
make yo' heart glad. . . .

The story he told was not new to Bigger. He had heard it from his mother's knee. It was a picture of life Bigger had killed within himself long before he killed Mary; that had been his first murder. He associated that story with that which he believed he had killed. For those who wanted to kill him did not believe he was human; he was not included in that picture of the Creation which the preacher told. That was the reason he had killed it. At this point, the author allows Bigger to come to the realization that he has killed in order to create a new world for himself. And he was now going to die for having made that creation for a person in his unique part of the human experience. The preacher was using a counterfeit image of man and his relationship to the Creation which was the official religious story. The social realism of Bigger's world called for a different religious view from the preacher's.

Unaware of Bigger's thoughts, the preacher droned on with his story of the Creation and of the Tree of Life, and the sinning of Adam and Eve and Cain and Able and the coming of Jesus who now makes it possible for man to have eternal life through the love of Jesus. "Son, look at me," the preacher pleaded as Bigger held his

172

head in his hands. "Son, promise me yuh'll stop
hatin' long enuff fer Gawd's love t' come inter
yo' heart." When Bigger did not respond, the
preacher rose, sighed, and drew from his pocket
a small wooden cross with a chain upon it, saying:

Look, son. Ah'm holdin' in mah hands a
wooden cross taken from a tree. A tree
is the worl', son. 'N' nailed t' this
tree is a sufferin' man. Tha's whut life
is, son. Sufferin'. How kin yuh keep
from b'lieving the word of Gawd when Ah'm
holdin' befo' yo' eyes the only thing tha'
gives meanin' t' yo' life? Here, lemme
put it roun' yo' neck. When yuh git alone,
look at this cross, son, 'n' b'lieve.

Just at the moment that the cross was touching his bare skin and he was feeling the words
of the preacher that life was flesh nailed to
the world, a longing spirit imprisoned in the
days of the earth, Jan Erlone, the Communist and
Mary Dalton's boyfriend, whom Bigger had tried
to cause to be charged with Mary's death, entered the cell. He explained to Bigger the impact the death of Mary and the attempt to accuse
him for her death had had upon him. But he
wanted to tell Bigger something. He had been
blind, he said, and he simply wanted to come to
tell Bigger he was not angry. Maybe Bigger had
his reasons for what he did, and maybe, in a
certain way, he, himself--Jan--was the guilty
one.

"Bigger, I've never done anything against you
and your people in my life," Jan tells him, "but
I'm a white man and it would be asking too much
to ask you not to hate me, when every white man
you see hates you." His face looks like the
others, he admitted, but the preacher came forward, "Is yuh Mistah Erlone?" he asked. When
Jan answered that he was, the preacher continued,

"Tha' wuz a mighty fine thing you jus' said,
suh. Ef anybody needs he'p, this po' boy sho
does. Ah'm Reverend Hammond."

Jan and the preacher shook hands, and the
young Communist went on to speak in terms of
salvation which surpassed the preacher's conventional words, as he said to Bigger, "I was in
jail grieving for Mary and then I thought of all
the black men who've been killed, the black men
who had to grieve when their people were snatch-
ed from them in slavery and since slavery. . . .
and I said 'I'm going to help that guy if he
lets me.'"

"May Gawd in heaven bless yuh, son," the
preacher said to Jan, and for the first time in
his life, Bigger looked at a white face and saw
an honest face. This white man believed in him,
and although he felt guilty again, he felt so in
a different sense now. The white man had come
up to him and made a declaration of friendship
that would make other men hate Jan, but a small
particle of the "looming mountain of white hate
had rolled down the slope, stopping at his feet."
The word had become flesh, and, ironically, it
was not the Reverend Hammond--despite his most
sincere efforts--who had "converted" Bigger. It
was the words of one who showed--not preached--
that he could love someone who had despitefully
used him. As if the author feared that his
readers might not fully understand which man was
more able to help Bigger, Reverend Hammond
quickly dropped his humility toward Jan and assumed that part of the black preacher Wright
seemed to dislike most. He spoke militantly,
but deferring, if that is possible:

"Ah don't wanna break in 'n' meddle where
Ah ain' got no business, suh, but there
ain' no use draggin' no communism in this
thing, Mistah. Ah respecks yo' feelin's
powerfully, suh; but what yuh's astin' stirs

up more hate. Whut this po' boy needs
is understandin'."

The preacher had sensed that Jan's offer of
an attorney for Bigger involved a Communist lawyer. Bigger had to fight for the understanding
he needed, Jan told the preacher. And the contest of misunderstanding took the form of debate
between Jan and Hammond. "Ah'm wid yuh when yuh
wanna change men's hearts," the preacher said,
"but I can't go wid yuh when yuh wanna stir up
mo' hate." Bigger sat looking bewildered from
one to the other as they seemed to vie for his
fate, and Jan asked, "How on earth are you going
to change men's hearts when the newspapers are
fanning hate into them every day?" Reverend
Hammond answers confidently, "God can change
'em!" Jan turned to Bigger and again begged him
to let Max, the lawyer, help him. Bigger finally agreed, amazed that someone could believe in
him that much, and Max, the attorney from the
Labor Defenders entered the cell. Very shortly,
Buckley, the State's Attorney, also entered, and
immediately expressed the official position of
the State and, so far as Bigger was concerned,
for the whole white world. "What in hell you
Reds can get out of bothering with a black thing
like that, God only knows." he shouted to Max
and Jan. "Why in God's name couldn't they pick
out somebody decent to defend sometimes?" he
asked. The association has been made through the
dramatic sequence which brings Buckley, Max,
Jan, and Reverend Hammond into the cell. The
incongruity of the alignment is ironic; for the
preacher who represents the deepest emotional
social involvement of the black American, and in
this case the person who most sincerely wants to
help Bigger, finds himself allied with Buckley,
the bigoted State's Attorney, in his condemnation of the Communists who only stir up trouble.

When Bigger's family comes to see him in the
cell, his shame discomforts him, as his mother

175

expresses her grief at his predicament. "I'll be out of here in no time," he says, trying to comfort her. Characteristically, she pours out her heart in hearing of all of the family, friends, the Communists, and the law enforcement officers in the cell, and the pathetic insufficiency of her whole religious orientation rings throughout the building. She kneels at Bigger's feet, looks upward and mourns:

"I'm praying for you, son. That's all I can do now," she said. "The Lord knows I did all I could for you and your sister and brother. I scrubbed and washed and ironed from morning till night, day in and day out, as long as I had strength in my old body. I did all I know how, son, and if I left anything undone, it's just 'cause I didn't know. It's just 'cause you poor old ma couldn't see, son. When I heard the news of what happened, I got on my knees and turned my eyes to God and asked Him to let me bear your burden if I did wrong by you. Honey, your poor old ma can't do nothing now. I'm old and this is too much for me. I'm at the end of my rope. Listen, son, your poor old ma wants you to promise her one thing. . . . Honey, when ain't nobody round you, when you alone, get on your knees and tell God everything. Ask Him to guide you. That's all you can do now. Son, promise me you'll go to Him."

"Ahmen!" the preacher intoned fervently.

"Forget me, Ma."

"Son, I'm worried about you. I can't help it. You got your soul to save. I won't be able to rest easy as long as I'm on this earth if I thought you had gone away from us without asking God for help. Bigger, we had a hard time in this world,

but through it all, we been together,
ain' we?"

"Yessum," he whispered.

"Son, there's a place where we can be together again in the great bye and bye.
God's done fixed it so we can. He's fixed
a meeting place for us, a place where we
can live without fear. No matter what
happens to us here, we can be together in
God's heaven. Bigger, your old ma's a-
begging you to promise her you'll pray."

"She's tellin' yuh right son," the preacher
said.

"Forget me, Ma," Bigger said.

"Don't you want to see your old ma again,
son?"

Slowly, he stood up and lifted his hands
and tried to touch his mother's face and
tell her yes; and as he did so something
screamed deep down in him that it was a
lie, that seeing her after they killed him
would never be. But his mother believed;
it was her last hope; it was what had kept
her going through the long years. And she
was now believing it all the harder because
of the trouble he had brought upon her.
His hands finally touched her face and he
said with a sigh (knowing that it would
never be, knowing that his heart did not
believe, knowing that when he died, it
would be over, forever):

"I'll pray, Ma."

Bigger does not intend to pray, he has not
changed his mind about his mother's religion.
He knows it will not save him, no matter how
hard he prays. But he has realized for the first

177

time that he is not alone in his misery; that
Jan and Max--total strangers--care enough to try
to help him, and that his family and his friends
are doing all they can for him. Reverend Hammond serves merely as a sincere stereotype of
the good minister whose religion offers nothing
useful to the people who place so much trust in
it. Bigger is not a believer, but his mother is,
and it is her well-being which needs to be safe-
guarded. And it is to a certain extent. In a
pathetic display of family affection, Bigger's
mother asked his sister, Vera, and his brother,
Buddy, to put their arms around their brother.
As they stand in the middle of the floor of the
cell, crying with their arms locked around Bigger, his mother mumbles a prayer, to which the
preacher chants:

> "Lord, here we is, maybe for the last
> time. You gave me these children, Lord,
> and told me to raise 'em. If I failed,
> Lord, I did the best I could. (Ahmen!)
> These poor children's been with me a
> long time and they's all I got. Lord,
> please let me see 'em again after the sor-
> row and suffering of this world! (Hear her,
> Lawd!) Lord, please let me see 'em where
> I can love 'em in peace. Let me see 'em
> again beyond the grave! (Have mercy, Jesus!)
> You said You'd heed prayer, Lord, and I'm
> asking this in the name of Your son."

> "Ahmen 'n' Gawd bless yuh, Sistah Thomas,"
> the preacher said.

We are leaving you with God now, Bigger's
mother tells him and they prepare to leave him
to his fate. They take their arms from around
him, silently, slowly, and turn their faces away,
as if their weakness makes them ashamed in the
presence of powers greater than themselves.
Thus, the author reduces to little more than a
tearful stylistic scene the disappointing power of the preacher and his religion. He has led

178

the family into praying for their loved one; he has prayed for him; he has given Bigger a crucifix to place around his neck. But he can do no more. No one can; but at least the Communists are prepared to fight for his life on the same terms that the prosecution will fight. They hold whatever hope there is, and that actually is none. But they are more equal than the Thomases and Reverend Hammond to the powers that well electrocute Bigger for his crime.

The author does not suggest a way the essence of the black church can help persons in Bigger Thomas' case. But even in the practice of the religion, outside uses of it for helping persons in trouble, the spokesmen for Communism understand the brotherhood of man and the commonality of human distress better than the church. They forgive; they love those who hate them; they struggle with the forces of oppression. The church turns away from even that degree of understanding, for as Reverend Hammond has made clear, Communists only stir up trouble. But he has no alternative to offer to Bigger Thomas. The rejection of the black man and his religion in the novel is devastating. The impotency of the preacher has been the vehicle through which that rejection has been accomplished.

CHAPTER 8 . . . . JAMES BALDWIN: Preachers
Without Love

> "I underwent, during the summer
> that I became fourteen, a pro-
> longed religious crisis. I
> use the word 'religious' in
> the common, and arbitrary,
> sense, meaning that I then
> discovered God, His saints and
> angels, and His blazing Hell.
> And since I had been born in a
> Christian nation, I accepted
> this Deity as the only one.
> I supposed Him to exist only
> within the walls of a church--
> in fact, of our church--and I
> also supposed that God and
> safety were synonymous. The
> word 'safety' brings us to the
> real meaning of the word 'reli-
> gious' as we use it."

> James Baldwin, The Fire Next
> Time

James Baldwin (1924-   ) is the most significant
Afro-American writer of the post-World War II
period. He has lived in his native New York City
and in Paris, France, throughout his career, and
has advanced black literature between the appearance of Richard Wright's Native Son and the dynamic American Civil Rights Movement and into
the 1970s. Baldwin has expressed his response
to his life and times in the short study, the
essay, the novel, and the drama. Some of his
most significant publications include the novels
Go Tell It on the Mountain (1953); Giovanni's
Room (1956); Another Country (1962); Tell Me How
Long the Train's Been Gone (1967); and If Beale
Street Could Talk (1974); the short story collection Going to Meet the Man (1965); the collection of essays, Notes of a Native Son (1955)

and <u>Nobody Knows My Name</u> (1961); and the dramas,
<u>Blue for Mister Charlie</u> (1964); and <u>The Amen
Country</u> (1968). The two dramas and parts of
<u>Go Tell It on the Mountain</u> provide the images of
the preacher for this study.

   <u>Go Tell It on the Mountain</u> explores the motivations, defenses, and pretensions of Gabriel
Grimes, store-front preacher who assists with
ministerial duties at the Temple of the Fire
Baptized Church in Harlem. John Grimes, his
14-year-old step-son and protagonist of the novel,
has reached the age of accountability and sexual awareness at the same time. His chronological age requires him to become converted to the
religious ethic of his fathers. The ugly and
illegitimate youth wants to believe it is his
heritage and responsibility to become a "saint"
in that religion, but the novel's tension devel-
ops around the youth's conscious rejection of
that ethic; for he hates his step-father, even
as the older man hates him, and believes a true
conversion will rid him of the hatred he knows
is a sin in a rational view of the religion he
is expected to follow blindly. John wants a different religion--a belief in conduct and ritual
that is foreign to his father and the other
"saints." He wants to find love, not merely in
the dull responsibility of bringing children into the world--especially black, ugly children
who, though literally legitimate, cannot find
fulfillment in the world in which they have been
born. Loveless life and disappointments in love
and pride in evading romantic love yield an un-
acceptable life. Yet, persons who suffer from
all of these human experiences make up the church
and its "saints." They have escaped into a false
paradise in which they delude themselves into ac-
cepting the unnatural substitution of the church
for real life and self-fulfillment that human

beings must find. This circumstance is especially pathetic for preachers. They must not
impose such a vision of life upon the young men
of their progeny who stand at the threshhold of
self-realization. Certainly, those are the fo-
cuses upon the preacher in Go Tell It on the
Mountain and in The Amen Corner. The essence of
Blues for Mister Charlie is broader and less per-
sonally motivated, as its preacher faces love-
lessness not through his own volition. Like
Richard Wright's Dan Taylor in "Fire and Cloud,"
Baldwin's Meridian Henry's strength in Blues lies
in his public commitment, even if it is motivated
by his private losses of his wife and son. He
becomes the realized militant preacher of the
mid-century that Wright envisioned a generation
earlier, but Baldwin's seems so much more plaus-
ible because his Meridian Henry enjoys the benefits of a nation's knowledge of the Civil Rights
marches that Dan Taylor's generation could only
imagine.

Go Tell It On The Mountain

    The Temple of the Fire Baptized Church is
not the biggest church in Harlem, nor yet the
smallest, but John has been brought up to believe
it is the holiest and best. His father was a
head deacon who took up the collection and sometimes preached. His extraordinary stern religion
and uses of it to punish his wife and son and
attempt to atone for his own previous sins made
Gabriel Grimes an unpleasant and tormented character in the novel. He reflects, at least on
the surface, Father James, "a genial, well-fed
man with a face like a darker moon," who was the
pastor of the church. He preached on Pentecost
Sundays, led revivals in summer, annointed con-
verts and healed the sick. He is a minor character in the plot of the novel whose image becomes clear in one memorable incident that brings
a seminal reaction from John. He had "uncovered
sin in the congregation of the righteous" when

he learned that his nephew Elisha and Ella Mae, the granddaughter of praying Mother Washington, had been "walking disorderly." Because they had been seen holding hands in the park they were in danger of straying from the Truth. Stern Father James called the two young persons before the congregation and censored them. Elisha hung his head as Father James condemned him and the congregation murmured its approval. Ella Mae who had been beautiful to John when she was singing and testifying looked to him now like an ordinary girl. Father James told the congregation his role as pastor of the flock was not easy, for Almighty God had placed an awful responsibility upon his shoulders. God would ask an account from him one day for every soul in the flock. When he was hard it was because the Word was hard and the way of holiness was a hard way. There was no room in God's army for a coward heart, no crown awaiting him who put mother, or father, sister, or brother, sweetheart, or friend above God's will. When he explained these responsibilities of the pastor while censoring Elisha and Ella Mae, Father James exclaimed, "Let the church say amen to this!" and they cried, "Amen! Amen!" Clearly, this religion would not permit human love outside the stringent confines of pietism. Father James claimed that the Lord led him to give public warning to these young church members before it was too late. He knew they were sincere young people, dedicated to the service of the Lord. Because they were young they did not know the pitfalls Satan laid in their way. Father James said he knew sin was not in the minds of Elisha and Ella Mae just yet, but he also knew that sin was in the flesh and that should the young church members continue walking out alone together their secrets and laughter and touching of hands would surely lead to a sin beyond all forgiveness. After he scolded Elisha and Ella Mae that Sunday before the whole congregation, they no longer met each day after school nor spent Saturday afternoons wandering through

184

Central Park or lying on the beach. All that was over for them. Now if they should come together again at all, it would be for the purpose of wedlock in which they would have children who would be raised in the church.

This holy life created confusion in John Grimes' mind on his 14th birthday that would occupy the majority of action in Go Tell It on the Mountain. For as he became more keenly aware of his own physical development and the carnal desires that were beginning to arise naturally in his mind and body, John had made his decision: He would not be like his father and his father's fathers. He would have another life.

Father James enunciates the religious codes for the fundamentalist church in which the novel is set. And he shows his willingness to enforce this kind of morality. John's step-father, though, Gabriel Grimes, presents the more discussable images of the preacher that are consistent with the general content of this study. They appear in direct action and in flashbacks beginning shortly after his own conversion to Christianity and his decision that he had been called to preach. That part of his life took place down South, long before Gabriel came to Harlem to live. It was during a large revival meeting carried on by 24 evangelists from throughout the surrounding counties. The event was called the Twenty-Four Elders Revival Meeting because each preacher performed one night with the hope of trying to "shine before men and to glorify their heavenly father." Each was experienced and well-known. Gabriel was astonished and honored to be included among them. He was young in the faith. Only yesterday, he had been "lying, vomit-covered, in the gutters of sin." He felt his hand shake with fear as the invitation came to him.

Gabriel was to preach on the 12th night in order that the "war horses" among the preachers

might support him on either side of their num-
bers. The young preacher took his opportunity
seriously. He fasted on his knees before God
and did not cease praying day and night that God
might work through him and cause men to see the
Almighty's hand on them. His new wife, Deborah,
prayed and fasted with him. The evening he was
scheduled to preach, Gabriel and Deborah walked
together to the great lighted lodge hall, so
lately used as a dance hall, that had been rented because it was the only building in the black
community that could accommodate the large audiences. The service had already begun as they
entered. After asking his wife to sit near so
he could see her as he preached, Gabriel turned
to walk up the long aisle to the pulpit. The
other preachers were already there--big, comfortable, ordained men. They smiled and nodded as
he mounted the pulpit steps. One explained the
other preachers were "just gettin' these folks
warmed up for you, boy, want to see you make them
holler tonight." Gabriel smiled and knelt at
his throne-like chair to pray and thought again,
as he had been thinking for the past 11 nights,
how much he wanted to make good of his opportunity to perform well as a preacher. When the
Scripture lesson had been read, the testimonies
spoken, the songs sung, and the collection taken,
Gabriel was introduced by the elder who had
preached the previous night. He found himself on
his feet moving toward the pulpit where the great
Bible awaited him. He did not begin with a "shout"
song or with a fiery testimony. Instead, he
started in a voice that trembled a little and
asked the congregation to look with him at the
sixth chapter of Isiah and fifth verse which he
asked Deborah to read aloud: "Then said I, woe
is me for I am undone, because I am a man of unclean lips, and I dwell in the midst of unclean
lips, for mine eyes have seen the king, the Lord
of Hosts." With all eyes on him, Gabriel began
his sermon:

These words had been uttered by the
prophet Isaiah who had been called the
eagle-eyed because he had looked like
the dark centuries and foreseen the birth
of Christ. It was Isaiah also who had
prophesied that a man should be as a
hiding-place from the wind and tempest,
Isaiah who had described the way of holiness, saying that the parched ground
should become a pool, and the thirsty
lands springs of water: the very desert
should rejoice, and blossom as a rose.
It was Isaiah who had prophesied saying:
'Unto us a child is born, unto us a son
is given; and the government shall be
upon his shoulder.' This was the man
who God had raised in righteousness,
whom God had chosen to do many mighty
things, yet this man, beholding the
vision of God's glory, had cried out:
'Woe is me!'

One woman in the congregation cried out,
"Tell it!" and Gabriel explained that there was
a lesson in the story about Isaiah for all people.
For if they had never made this cry they had never known salvation. If they had failed to live
with this cry hourly, daily, in the midnight, and
in the light of the noonday sun, salvation had
left all people and their feet were on the way to
hell. Whenever we cease to tremble before Him,
he told his congregation, we turn from the way of
God. He paused for a moment to mop his brow and
his own heart within him was great with fear and
trembling. But a growing power of confidence
moved him forward with his sermon:

For let us remember that the wages of
sin is death; that it is written, and
cannot fail, the soul that sinneth, it
shall die. Let us remember that we are
born in sin, in sin did our mothers con-
ceive us--sin reigns in all our members,
sin in the foul heart's natural liquid,

sin looks out of the eye, amen, and leads
to folly, sin sits on the tongue, and
leads to murder. Yes! Sin is the only
heritage of the natural man, sin be-
queathed us by a natural father, that
falling Adam, whose apple sickens and
will sicken all generations living, and
generations unborn; it was sin that drove
the son of the morning out of heaven, sin
that drove Adam out of Eden, sin that
caused Cain to slay his brother, sin that
built the Tower of Babel, sin that caused
the fire to fall on Sodom . . . .

His sermon followed the pattern of the traditional revival performance of the old-time
preacher. It moved from original sin, through
the plan for salvation, to the death of Jesus on
the cross. The congregation supported Gabriel
throughout. All of the elders smiled at him and
one said, "That was mighty fine, boy. Mighty
fine." At a spectacular dinner that came at the
close of the series of meetings, Gabriel joined
the other preachers in the celebration dinner.
At first the young preacher felt unworthy among
these men he considered his elders in the faith
and in the profession of preaching, but he came
to disdain them for their worldliness. They
were not like those holy prophets of old who grew
thin and naked in the service of the Lord. These
men had grown fat and their dress was rich. Moreover, they revelled in their misuse of the women
of the church. Gabriel dreamed, the night after
the dinner, that two demons—old friends he had
known but saw no more—came to his bed. They
were drinking and gambling and offering women he
had known before, too. They were so real that
he could nearly touch them, and his pagan body
stiffened and flamed as the women laughed, asking
why he remained in his narrow bed when they waited for him. The dream was the manifestation of
the life Gabriel had chosen for himself as he
gained high status in the company of the com-

munity's preachers. He had chosen a sinless life
as he understood sin.

At this point, Gabriel experiences his major
temptation and fall. He becomes infatuated with
Esther, a voluptuous, young woman who works in
the same household in which he is employed. Each
night, he sees her walk off from work into the
dark on a young man's arm, and their voices and
laughter floated back to mock him. His marriage
to Deborah is totally joyless. It was simply a
matter of two persons who believed they should
and could like a pure life. She had been raped
by some white men when she was a teenager, and
the community no longer considered her a candi-
date for worthy home membership in the society
as a wife and mother. Gabriel had married her
out of pity and as assurance that with her he
could live the pietistic life his religion required. Esther served as a sharp contrast to
Deborah. She lived with her mother and step-
father who ran a bawdy house. People like her
and her family seldom came to church; but her
vitality and sensuality troubled Gabriel. He
told himself he felt sorry for her; that he
wanted to convert her to his form of Christianity. He invited her to the church one night
when he was going to preach and she came. He
invited the temptation that would cause him to
"fall from grace," part knowingly and part in
innocence of the possible consequences.

Just before the presiding preacher introduced Gabriel to that congregation, Esther and
her mother entered the church. When he saw the
beautiful young woman, totally incompatible with
the other women in the church and representing
the fallacy that he thought he had conquered in
taking on his exaggerated piety, something ex-
ploded in Gabriel's heart. Esther moved directly to a seat in the back of the congregation
without looking at the preacher at all, although
he knew immediately that she had seen him. In a

moment, he imagined, his sermon would bring her to her knees at the altar and he would bring her into the service of the Lord. Esther wore a blue hat, trimmed with many ribbons, and a heavy wine-red dress. Her mother, much larger and darker, wore great gold earrings. The two women sat "like sisters of sin, living alike a living defiance of the drab sanctity of the saints." Deborah looked back at them, and as she did Gabriel realized for the first time how unattractive and wholly undesirable his wife was. He felt his hand which held the Bible begin to sweat and tremble. He thought of the joyless groaning of his marriage bed. He hated Deborah.

Although this particular image of the preacher in Go Tell It on the Mountain is told through Gabriel's memory, it is vivid--"like the memory of a storm." The moment he raised his head from the customary prayer before his sermon and looked out over the faces again, his tongue was loosed and he was filled with the power of the Holy Ghost. He preached with such exuberance that night that it was said that he set a standard for visiting evangelists for a generation to come. Many years later when Esther and Deborah both were dead and Gabriel was leaving the South, people remembered this sermon and the gaunt, possessed young man who had preached it. He took his text form the 18th Chapter of the Second Book of Samuel, the story of young Ahimaaz who ran too soon to bring the tidings of battle to King David. Before he ran he was asked by Job: "Wherefore wilt thou run, my son, seeing that thou hast no tidings ready?" And when Ahimaaz reached King David who yearned to know the fate of his head-long son Absalom, he could only say: "I saw a great tumult but I knew not what it was."

Gabriel preached that this was the story of all who failed to wait on the counsel of the Lord; those who made themselves wise in their own conceit and ran before they had the tidings ready.

He said this was a story of innumerable shep-
herds who failed in their arrogance to feed the
hungry sheep; of many a father and mother who
gave to their children not bread but a stone; of
those who offered not the truth of God but the
tinsel of the world. Every brother and sister
beneath the sound of his voice that night had
seen the destruction that had been caused by
such a "lamentable unripeness," Gabriel preached.
Some had heard it on the streets, in the fields;
others had heard it in their homes; some had
heard it from the pulpit. But none should wait
any longer; instead they should rise that day
and bring down the mighty, establishing the vengeance that God had claimed. He counseled his
congregation, though, that he who believeth
should not make haste, although sometimes the
road was rocky. Did they think sometimes that
God forgot?, he asked, and continued:

> Oh, fall on your knees and pray for
> patience; fall on your knees and pray
> for faith; fall on your knees and pray
> for overcoming power to be ready on the
> day of his soon appearing to receive
> the crown of life for God did not for-
> get, no word proceeding from his mouth
> could fail. Better to wait like Job
> through all of the days of our appointed
> time until our change comes than to rise
> up unready before God speaks. For if we
> but wait humbly before him he will speak
> glad tidings to our souls; if we but wait
> our change will come. And that in an in-
> stant, in the twinkling of an eye--we will
> be changed one day from this corruption
> into uncorruptibility forever, caught up
> with him beyond the clouds and these are
> the tidings we now must bear to all the
> nations: another son of David was hung
> from a tree and he who knows not the
> meaning of that tumult shall be damned
> forever in hell! Brother, Sister, you

191

may run, but the day is coming when the
King will ask: 'What are the tidings
that you bear?'   And what will you say
on that great day if you know not of the
death of his son.

As he moved into the invitation of sinners
to accept Jesus Christ on the basis of the stir-
ring sermon he had just preached, Esther nor her
mother seemed inclined to come down the long
aisle to the mercy seat. For a moment Gabriel
was filled with holy rage that Esther, in particular, could stand so brazen in the congregation of the righteous and refuse to bow her head.
He felt drained and sick; he was soaking wet and,
he smelled the odor of his own body. Deborah began singing and beating a tambourine in the
front of the congregation, watching her husband.
He felt suddenly like a helpless child, wanting
to hide forever and cease crying. Esther and
her mother left during the singing for they had
come only to hear him preach. He could not
imagine what they were saying among themselves
or thinking. But he did remember to tell himself that he would see her again tomorrow.

The next morning Esther came into the yard
saying, "Good morning, Reverend. I sure didn't
look to see you today. I reckoned you'd be all
worn out after that sermon--does you always
preach as hard as that?" He explained that he
preaches the way the Lord leads him. She agreed
that it was a mighty fine sermon; that she and
her mother were glad they had come out to hear
him. At the moment, Gabriel Grimes was sincere
in the role which he believed that the preacher
was expected to play in the relationship between
him and Esther. She offended him because she
was so brazen in her sin and that was all. He
prayed for her soul which would one day find itself naked and speechless before the judgement
bar of Christ. Later, she told him that she had
pursued him and that his eyes had left her not a

moment's peace. "That weren't no reverend looking at me them mornings in the yard," she had
said to him. "You looked at me just like a man,
like a man who hadn't never heard of the Holy
Ghost." But he continued to believe that the
Lord had laid her like a burden on his heart and
he carried her in his heart praying for her and
exhorting her to bring her soul to God. Esther
did not look upon Gabriel Grimes as God's minister but as a "purty man."

The author explains Gabriel's fall in dramatic terms:

So he had fallen: For the first time
since his conversion, for the last time
in his life. Fallen: he and Esther in
the white folks' kitchen, the light burning beside the sink. Fallen indeed: time
was no more, and sin, death, Hell, the
judgement were blotted out. There was
only Esther, who contained in her narrow
body all mystery and all passion, and who
answered all his need. Time, snarling so
swiftly past, had caused him to forget the
clumsiness, and sweat and dirt of their
first coupling; how his shaking hands un-
dressed her, standing where they stood,
how her dress fell at length like a snare
about her feet; how his hands tore at her
undergarments so that the naked, vivid
flesh might meet his hands; how she protested: 'Not here, not here'; how he
worried, in some buried part of his mind,
about the open door, about the sermon he
was to preach, about his life, about Deborah; how the table got in their way, how
his collar, until her fingers loosened it,
threatened to choke him; how they found
themselves on the floor at last, sweating
and groaning and locked together; locked
away from all others, all heavenly or

human help. Only they could help each other. They were all alone in the world.

Their torrid love affair lasted for nine days before Gabriel came to his senses and "God gave him the power to tell her this could not be." Esther took his decision casually, in near-amusement. She could not complicate her own way of life by the confusions and contradictions which bothered him. She believed that life was intended to be simple. Gabriel understood that she was sorry for him because he was always worrying. Sometimes when they were together he tried to tell her what he felt, how the Lord would punish them for the sin they were commiting. But she would not listen. "You ain't in the pulpit now," she would tell him. "You's here with me. Even a Reverend's got the right to take off his clothes <u>sometime</u> and act like a natural man." Gabriel prayed that Esther would never come to hear him preach again and he thanked God that the situation had not been worse. Naturally, he prayed that God would forgive him and never let him fall again. But what frightened him most and what kept him more than ever on his knees was the knowledge that once having fallen, nothing would be easier than to fall again. For having possessed Esther, the carnal man awoke seeing the possibility of conquest everywhere. He was made to remember that although he was holy, he was yet young. The women who had wanted him wanted him still. He had only to stretch out his hand and take what he wanted. Even the sisters in the church. He struggled to wear out his visions in the marriage bed and he struggled to awaken Deborah for whom daily his hatred grew. When in the spring Esther told him she was going to have his baby, Gabriel vowed that he was ill-prepared to take on the responsibility for their child. Esther was going to have his baby; not Deborah, his wife. His only off-spring was in the womb of Esther who, to him, was no better than a harlot and yet, it was within her that the

194

seed of the prophet would be nourished. This particular image of the preacher enraged Gabriel.

As a holy man he was totally unprepared for the consequences of his brief love affair with Esther. Their positions were polar in his terms although they had loved freely and fully. Satan tempted him and he fell; he was not the first man who had been made to fall on account of a woman. Esther retorted that she was not the first girl who has been ruined by a holy man. Reacting angrily to the term "ruined," Gabriel asked how she could be ruined when she had been walking through the streets of the town like a harlot, "or kicking up your heels all over the pasture?" They argued violently. Esther knew she could tell Gabriel's wife and the church folks and everybody, and he threatened by re- minding her that few people would believe her. Enough folks would believe it to make it hard on him, she explained. She laughed sardonically as she pointed out to him, "but I ain't the holy one. You's a married man and you's a preacher-- who you think the folks is going to blame most?" When he explained that she knew he could not marry her, Esther admitted that Gabriel would not marry her even if he were free because he would not want her for his wife. Sure, she was all right for the night, for the dark where no one would see him "getting his holy life all dirtied up." She was just good enough to go out and have his baby somewhere in the woods but nothing more. Because this was the case, she did not want to be with him any more than he wanted to be with her. She did not want any man who was ashamed and scared. Such a man could do her no good. There was only one thing she wanted him to do. She had no desire to go through the town and tell everybody about the Lord's anointed. For to do so would make her mother and father know what a fool she had been. No, she was not ashamed of herself but she was ashamed of Gabriel. He had made her feel a shame she had never felt

before. "I'm shamed before my God to let somebody make me cheap like you done done," she
hurled at him. She wanted to go some place and
have her baby and think the whole matter out of
her mind. She thought this was an easy enough
solution for Gabriel. "I guess it takes a holy
man to make a girl a real whore," she says to
Gabriel in ultimate derision.

Esther wrote once from Chicago, ending her
letter with these words:

> What I think is, I made a mistake, that's
> true, and I'm paying for it now. But
> don't you think you ain't going to pay
> for it--I don't know when and I don't know
> how, but I know you going to be brought
> low one of these fine days. I ain't holy
> like you are, but I know right from wrong.
> I am going to have my baby and I'm going
> to bring him up to be a man and I ain't
> going to read to him out of no Bibles and
> I ain't going to take him to hear no
> preaching. If he don't drink nothing but
> moonshine all his natural days he be a
> better man than his daddy.

Esther died during childbirth, and her un-
timely death placed a deep and abiding guilt upon
Gabriel that followed him wherever he went. He
believed he saw his guilt in everybody's eyes.
When he stood in the pulpit to preach they looked
at him as though he had no right to be there.
When souls came weeping to the altar he scarcely
dared to rejoice, remembering that soul who had
not bowed, whose blood, it might be, would be
required of him in judgement. Bearing this extraordinary guilt, he moved to Harlem where he
was no longer a minister in charge of the congregation but one of the two deacons in the church
where he preached upon occasion when Father James
needed a substitute.

This religion, then, is the heritage John Grimes will earn as he becomes converted to the tradition of his fathers. The novel's principal action revolves around the agony of the teenage male who struggles, with the prayers of the "saints," to break through his imagined sins into the community of his father's joyless life of presumed purity and painful guilt for his incapacity to love honestly in his youth. Separating Gabriel Grimes from his role as father and husband in his own family, one gains a memorable image of the black preacher. That image strains under the tensions of a need to cleanse himself of the larger sin of rejecting the essence of humanity that plagues the proud preacher. It is, further, the personification of the preacher whose pulpit rhetoric and prescriptions he imposes upon his needs as a human being who assumes a non-human role in a profession that cries out for uncommon human sensitivities. It is the old story, fairly traditional in Afro-American literature, of the preacher who takes literally his responsibility to preach a gospel he cannot live on a personal basis.

The novel is John's. It opens on the day of his necessity to choose moral responsibility. He is expected to become a preacher. For that reason, most of the emphasis of the plot is placed on his conversion. However, John does not want to become the kind of preacher Father James and Gabriel are. Not as he sees them. His basis for rejecting their image of the preacher lies primarily in their life-denying attitude toward those aspects of the human condition that seem most important to the adolescent John at the time we meet him in the novel. They are equally as important to the author and they seem to be the aspects of the human condition he celebrates rather than the need to be saved from original sin in the conventional sense of the term. Go Tell It on the Mountain is a complex work, employing far-reaching metaphors and paradigms of

the black American experience. For purposes of
this study, though, we have concentrated upon
Father James and Gabriel Grimes--principally the
latter--as the preachers in the culture of which
they are an integral part.

The Amen Corner

    In his notes for The Amen Corner, Baldwin
writes that the first line he put on paper as he
started to write the play was the central character's line in the third act: "It's an awful
thing to think about, the way love never dies."
He writes that at the time he was remembering the
"terrifying desolation" of his own private life
and the great burdens his father, a minister,
carried. "I was old enough by now, at last, to
recognize the nature of the dues he had to pay,
old enough to wonder if I could possibly have
paid them, old enough, at last to know that I had
loved him and had wanted him to love me," Baldwin
explains. His racial vision of the black experience in America had taught him to recognize that
any sensitive black father would be terrified at
what he knew was surely going to happen to his
son. And he had come to realize the strategems
his mother and other women had been forced to
use in order to save their children from the destruction they knew awaited their offspring just
outside the door. This consciousness brought him
to understand what Margaret Alexander, the central character in The Amen Corner, goes through
and what menaces her male child. She was a lady
preacher because society had left her no other
place to go but the ministry. Her sense of reality had been dictated by society's assumption
that she was inferior and her acceptance of that
verdict. She needed both human affirmation and
a vengeance against a society that circumscribed
her. Her only opportunity to strike back had
been expressed in her merciless piety, placing
her love--that which is real in the play--at the

mercy of her genuine and absolutely justifiable terror. This debilitating circumstance turns women like Margaret Alexander into tyrannical matriarchs who lose themselves and their progeny.

Margaret's husband, returning to her as he is dying, remembers her as a "fiery, fast-talking, little black woman" he had loved before poverty and fear had separated them. And it is that love of man for woman that becomes to the author a historical triumph of black people in the United States. They become torn on the pathetic dilemma of copious human love and compenastory religion. Their deepest strivings dramatize this mystification. The love and compassion affirm life and its fullness; the pietistic religion tries in vain to compensate for the life force. Specifically, Margaret Alexander learns the <u>true</u> keys to the kingdom and learns that the true kingdom is the kingdom of human love. As Baldwin expresses it, "that love is selfless, although only the self can lead one there." Accordingly, Margaret regains <u>herself</u> at the end of the play. Upon these bases, she cannot succeed as a preacher. It is the wrong place for her. The image, then, is neither redeeming nor wholesome. Instead, the play's strongest statement condemns the woman who loses her natural inclinations to love, motherhood, and successful marriage in order to live in and preside over a false paradise she believes is the kingdom of God's work on earth.

Sight and sound in the stage directions emphasize the conflict between the virtues of home for the mother, father, and son and those of the public ministry for the woman preacher. When the scrim rises, one sees the church dominated by the pulpit on a platform upstage where a throne-like chair stands. An immense Bible lies on the pulpit. Two collection plates--one brass and one straw--rest on the table. The church is on a level above the apartment in which Margaret

199

and her son live. The stage directions state
that the church dominates the family's living
quarters. As the curtain rises, there is a kind
of subdued row and humming out of which is heard
the music prologue, "The Blues Is Man," that
comes into a steady frolicking beat into the
church as the congregation sings in counterpoint:

One day I walked the lonesome road
The spirit spoke unto me
And filled my heart with love--
Yes, he filled my heart with love,
Yes, he filled my heart with love,
And he wrote my name above,
And that's why I thank God I'm in his care.

Visible contradiction places the church
above the home, and audible contradiction places
the love-sick blues alongside the Christian's
song of witness. One can hardly tell the difference between the two strains that reflect the
ethnic tension. Within this denial of wholeness
of human spirit, Margeret Alexander takes the
text for the sermon she will preach to her congregation: "The Lord God Almighty--the King of
Kings, Amen!"--had sent out the word, "Set thine
house in order, for thou shalt die and not live.
And King Hezakiah turned his face to the wall."
She explains that when the king got his message
to set his house in order he did not do as some
people were doing. He did not go running to a
spiritualist; he did not spend a lot of money on
some fancy doctor; he did not break his neck trying to get himself committed to Belleview Hos-
pital. He sent for the Prophet Isaiah, although
the king was extremely rich. He could have had
a lot of preachers around, "puffed up and riding
around in chariots just like they do today."
Most of them, she said, were stealing from the
poor. The king did not call on any of them. He
called on Isaiah because that prophet lived a
holy life, and in that Bible story lay the essence of the morning's sermon:

200

The world can't come to you if you don't
live holy. This way of holiness is a hard
way. I know some of you think Sister
Margaret's too hard on you. She don't
want you to do this and she won't let you
do that. Some of you say, 'Ain't no harm
in reading the funny papers.' But children, yes, there's harm in it. While
you're reading them funny papers, your
mind ain't on the Lord. And if your mind
ain't stayed on him, every hour of the day,
Satan's going to cause you to fall. Amen;
some of you say, 'Ain't no harm in me
working for a liquor company. I ain't
going to be drinking the liquor, I'm just
going to be driving the truck!' But a
saint of God ain't got no business deliver-
ing liquor to folks all day--how are you
going to spend all day helping folks into
hell and then think you are going to come
here in the evening and help folks into
heaven? It can't be done. The Word tells
me, no man can serve two masters!

Most human beings hardly wish to become
saints, as a test of Margaret's kind of pietism
shows during the same service. Ida Jackson, a
young mother in the congregation, responds to
Sister Moore--Margaret's chief associate--who
asks for persons who want the prayers of the
church to come to the altar. The woman comes
holding her sick baby. She explains the baby
cannot keep food in his stomach and cries all
night. "Sister, I done lost one child already,
please pray the Lord to make this baby well,"
she implores Margaret, who kindly assures her:
"Don't fret, little sister, Don't fret this
morning. The Lord is mighty to save. This here
is a holy ghost station." Margaret asks Ida
Jackson about her husband and the young woman
explains he has become evil and bitter and does
not want to hear anyone mention the name of the
Lord in his presence. She still believes in her

religion, though, and is trying to live a life
that will be pleasing to her Lord. "Maybe the
Lord wants you to leave that man," Margaret
pushes, and Ida replies, "No, He don't want that!"
As the congregation hums "Deep River," Margaret
prays with the child in her arms and her head
uplifted:

> Dear Lord, we come before you this morning
> to ask you to look down and bless this
> woman and her baby. Touch his little
> body, Lord, and heal him and drive out
> them tormenting demons. Raise him up,
> Lord, and make him a good man and a
> comfort to his mother. Yes, we know you
> can do it, Lord. You told us if we just
> call, trusting in your promise, you'd be
> sure to answer and all these blessings we
> ask in the name of our Father.

Ida Jackson precipitates Margaret's "fortunate fall" from the false paradise she has established for herself, and provides the means
through which she can restore herself to "original joy." Margaret's teenage son, David, wants
to pursue his own life, free of his mother's
selection for the two of them. Their house needs
to be set in order. David has been playing the
piano in the church, but he wants to move away
from this limitation. He is growing beyond
childhood. The first argument between mother
and son comes as Margaret announces her plan to
take David with her to Philadelphia to visit
Mother Phillips. She is the woman preacher
Margaret and her son lived with when she divorced her husband. David rebels. He objects
to taking a week off from music school to visit
someone he hardly remembers. Margaret, sensing
she may be losing control over the youth, tells
his she does not know what the school can teach
him. "You got a natural gift for music. . . .
The Lord give it to you, you didn't learn it in
no school," she argues. Their argument brings

202

Margaret the chance to chastise David for seeming to lose interest in the church and in his growing away from her supervision: "Where was you last night? You wasn't out to tarry service and don't nobody know what time you come in." David lies, "I had to go--downtown. We--having exams next week in music school and--I was studying with some guys I go to school with."

Luke Alexander, Margaret's estranged husband and her son's father, enters the drama at this point. As the "gentleman caller" returning to his wife's life, his presence and influence bring the agent for Margaret's banishment from her false paradise. She resists his interruption of her pietistic life at first with all her fervor:

> MARGARET: Why did you come here? You ain't never brought me nothing but trouble, you come to bring me more trouble? Luke-- I'm glad to see you and all but--I got to be going away this afternoon. I stay busy all the time around this church. David, he stays busy too--and he's coming with me this afternoon.

> LUKE: Well, honey, I'm used to your going. I done had ten years to get used to it. But, David--David, you can find a couple of minutes for your old man, can't you? Maybe you'd like to come out with me sometime--we could try to get acquainted.

The Alexander family discusses their affairs in David's hearing for the first time. He learns that Luke did not desert his family as Margaret had led him to believe. Margaret's response to her new challenge is, at first, automatic and predictable. She says the Lord made her leave Luke a long time ago because he was a sinner, "and the Lord ain't told me to

203

stop doing my work just because he's come the way all sinners come." She will relate to Luke only as his preacher trying to save his soul. Although Margaret tries valiantly to disassociate herself from Luke, other than as a sinner who may come to her church for salvation, her chief lieutenants begin to question her leadership as a result of her husband's coming to the church. They scrutinize Margaret in a new light. "She act like she way above all human trouble," Sister Boxer says, and continues:

> "Last Sunday she acted like she didn't think that man was good enough to touch the hem of that white robe of her'n. And you know, that ain't no way to treat a man who knowed <u>one</u> time what you was like with no robe on."

Another objects to the attack on the pastor, and Sister Boxer retorts:

> "Well, its the truth. I'm bearing witness to the truth. I reckon I always thought of Sister Margaret like she's been born holy. Like she hadn't never had no real temptations."

Neither woman is actually sympathetic; each is disappointed in finding their pastor is a human being. Margaret is assailed on her two most vulnerable sides: the romantic love for Luke she has quelled for ten years by entering the ministry and her love for her son who is now moving out of her control. David had learned that his father is playing piano in a jazz combo in Manhattan and has been going out to hear him play. Father and son have met. Margaret's worst fear has come to pass. She has taught David music is an evil that can lead him to ruin unless he uses his talent "for the Lord." She hopes to keep her son bound to her. That alliance also keeps him away from romantic love. "Every time I--even when I tried to make it with a girl--something kept saying, Maybe this is a sin," David tells his father. And Luke speaks to him the case for love in the drama:

> The most terrible time in a man's life, David, is when he's done lost everything that held him together--its just gone and he can't find it. The whole world just get to be a great big empty basin. And it just as hollow as a basin when you strike it with your fist. Then that man start going down. If don't no hand reach out to help him, that man goes under. You know, David, it don't take much to hold a man together. A man can lose a whole lot, might look to everybody else that he done lost so much that he ought to want to be dead, but he can keep on--he can even die with his head up, hell, as long as he get one thing. That one thing is _him_, David, who he is inside--and son, I don't believe no man ever got to that without somebody loved him. Somebody _looked_ at him, looked _way_ down in him and spied him way down there and showed him to himself--and started pulling, a-pulling of him up--so he could live.

Luke is dying of tuberculosis, but he re-deems his wife and his son by rejuvenating the memory of his marriage to Margaret. "We didn't get married because we loved God. We loved each other," he reminds his wife. When Margaret in-sists upon trying to save his soul, Luke taunts her with, "Is you got peace in your soul?" Speak-ing in the jargon of her image as a preacher, Margaret replies: "Yes! He done calmed the waters, He done beat back the powers of darkness, He done made me a new woman!" The reader learns through their dialogue that Margaret's life with Luke has paralleled Ida Jackson's. For, like the younger woman she tried to counsel, Margaret had

buried a young baby ten years earlier. That was
the time she swore to God she was going to
change her way of living. Luke blamed the death
of the baby on the young family's poverty. Yes,
he neglected them; he was drunk when he should
have been present and resourceful, but Luke refused to take the full responsibility for their
despair:

> I was there. I was there. Yes, I was
> drunk, but I was sitting at your bedside
> every day. Every time you come to your-
> self you looked at me and started scream-
> ing about how I'd killed our baby. Like
> I'd taken little Margaret and strangled
> her with my own two hands. Yes, I was
> drunk but I was waiting for you to call
> me. You never did. You never did.

Margaret has been forced into a painful new
examination of her own choices in life and their
consequences. Ida Jackson appears at the sleeping quarters, wearing a house dress and slippers.
She puts her hands to her face, moans, and falls
upon the altar. "Sister Margaret, you's a woman
of the Lord--you stay in communion with the Lord.
Why He take my baby from me? Tell me why He do
it?" Once more, Margaret recommends prayer and
trust. This time, Ida Jackson rejects the religion Margaret has to offer. "I'm just a young
woman, I just want my man and my home and my
children," she cries. Margaret and her religion
can do nothing for her. Margaret's role as
preacher declines from this point in the drama.
David rejects her authority and her reliance
upon the language of the pulpit fails. How is
she going to preach to others when her "man is
in there, dying," and her son is going out into
the world. Her placebo fails as she weeps:

> All these years I prayed as hard as I
> knowed how. I tried to put my treasure
> in heaven where couldn't nothing get at

it and take it away from me and leave
me alone. I asked the Lord to hold my
hand. I didn't expect that none of this
would ever rise to hurt me no more. And
all these years it just been waiting for
me, waiting for me to turn a corner. And
there it stand, my whole life, just like
I hadn't never gone nowhere. It's a awful
thing to think about the way love never
dies!

The church officers declare Sister Moore
their new pastor, one who prides herself on purity. She says she will go to God just as he
created her, for no man has ever "known" her.
Margaret has tried to live that life, but she
has failed in the face of forces she cannot control. Her's is a "fortunate fall," though; for
her last statement to the congregation that has
already ruefully rejected her for her humanity
carries a different message from that she has
tried to live by. She finally has her house in
order, as she tells the church:

Children. I'm just now finding out what
it means to love the Lord. It ain't all
in the singing and the shouting. It ain't
all in the reading of the Bible. (she
clenches her fist a little) It ain't
even--it ain't even--in running all over
everybody trying to get to heaven. To
love the Lord is to love all his children--
all of them, everyone!--and suffer with
them and rejoice with them and never count
the cost!

This uncertain life of reconciliation with
herself and the parts of her life she now realizes are essential negate an image of a preacher
that exaggerates piety and rejects human, personal love. The highly stylized practice of
Christianity that the drama illustrated cannot
compensate for the human affection the poorest

207

black family might enjoy. Ironically, seeking
to find some unique efficacy in that religious
practice only confuses the meanings of life, as
the cases of Ida Jackson and Margaret show.

Blues for Mister Charlie

Like many other Americans, James Baldwin
agonized over the bitter racial climate that
spread over the South following the Supreme
Court's decision in May, 1954, in Brown vs. Topeka, declaring that color discrimination in public education was unconstitutional. December 1,
1955, Rosa Parks was arrested in Montgomery,
Alabama, for refusing to give up her seat in the
front of a bus to a white man. The specific incident led to organization of the Montgomery Improvement Association and its protracted boycott
of the city's public service busses. The National Association for the Advancement of Colored
People initiated legal action that outlawed segregation in interstate travel, public education,
and public recreation. Martin Luther King, Jr.'s
name became a household word as a leader in organizations and movements determined to give
reality to those Constitutional Amendments that
had assured first-class citizenship for black
Americans nearly a century earlier. Reactions
from public officials and the White Citizens
Council brought on unprecedented racial tension
throughout the deep South, in particular. Con-
gress moved slowly to implement the edicts of
the federal courts. Lynching and economic pressures became the chief methods conservative
Southerners used to vitiate the growing effectiveness of the black civil rights movement and
the proliferation of organizations dedicated to
that purpose. Churches, the only free-standing
and independent institutions in the black community, became the impetus for the new incentive.
Every black community had its churches. They
were uniquely unrelated, in most cases, to white

Southern Protestants who, before the beginning
of the Civil War, had split on geographic lines
over slavery. The churches, then, became the
strength of the populist movement--the staging
areas for rallies, "sit-ins," demonstrations--
and the source for the movements' leaders and
followers. The black preacher added significant
dimensions to his traditional role, enriched by
the peculiar nature of the church which was the
political base, the house of worship, the concert hall, and often the school for black Americans. That extraordinary institution--its
priesthood, its buildings, and its lay leaders--
became the target of the relentless hatred that
frustrated white Southern Protestants. Ironically, they had taught slaves Christianity with a
view toward lulling them into a passive view of
life that would accept little earthly privilege
and materials. They would sacrifice self-respect
for the possibility of reward in heaven. The
new militancy was anathema to the ruling order.

Those ironies of two ethnic groups living
by the same Bible and the same Constitution engage the interest of many black writers. Persons
caught up in the paradox transcend their personal dilemma and illustrate, in their aloneness,
the individual agony a principal actor in this
American drama faces. The "eternal" and "uni-
versal" aspects of the human condition this particular drama explores brings Lyle Britten, the
white storekeeper who is accused of killing
Richard Henry, into ethical confrontation with
Meridian Henry, Richard's father and the black
preacher in the community.

Baldwin wrote in his notes to Blues that he
feared he could not adequately represent in the
play his true feeling toward the problem the
Lyle Brittens of the nation create. He wrote:

That fear was that I would never be able
to draw a valid portrait of the murderer.

In life, obviously, such people baffle
and terrify me and, with one part of my
mind at least, I hate them and would be
willing to kill them. Yet, with another
part of my mind, I am aware that no man
is a villain in his own eyes. Something
in the man knows--must know--that what he
is doing is evil; but in order to accept
the knowledge the man would have to
change. What is ghastly and really almost
hopeless in our social situation now is
that the crimes we have committed are so
great and so unspeakable that the acceptance of this knowledge would lead, literally, to madness. The human being, then,
in order to protect himself, closes his
eyes, compulsively repeats his crimes,
and enters a spiritual darkness which no
one can describe.

Private and public committment motivate the
father. These two men and the agon their wills
present illustrate what Baldwin calls the "plague"
Christianity visits upon the nation. "Plague
Town, U.S.A." is the play's setting and the
present is "the present." That unspoken but
well-known curse, Baldwin believes possesses the
power to destroy every human relationship. The
preacher illuminates the human experience in the
topical play. Emmett Tell was among several
blacks who were lynched in the heat of the social
unrest. Baldwin's prototype of Till is the son
of Meridian Henry. This double entendre gives
the playwright a relationship to the murder he
cannot resist. It places the preacher at critical variance with the "law," the religion, and
the social custom of his time and place. The
play is dedicated to the memory of Mississippi
NAACP official Medgar Evers who was shot to
death outside his home in Jackson in 1953 and
to four young children who were killed when a
bomb destroyed a part of the 16th Street Baptist
Church in Birmingham that same year.

The play's stage setting dramatizes the dual society that is the social truth of the nation about which Baldwin writes. The multiple set provides opposite sides of a Southern street. The first two acts take place in the black church building and the third is enacted in the courthouse. The audience should always be aware during the first two acts of the dome of the courthouse and the American flag. During the final act the audience should always be aware of the steeple of the church and the cross. The church is divided by an aisle that serves to divide the community into two opposing religions--both called Christianity. One is White Town, the other Black Town. This tragic division of human beings represents to a large extent the national plague that troubles the playwright. Meridian Henry projects the best attitudes of Black Town; the speaking part in the play simply labeled "The State" validates the legal position of White Town. As the drama unfolds, Meridian Henry moves from a moderate religious and political thinker into the keeper and strange and highly complex metaphor of the Bible and the gun placed upon the altar in the black church in the United States. With unerring logic and shocking reminder, he relates that mid-20th century metaphor of the black experience with the original Colonial Pilgrims who carried their shotguns to their meeting houses to protect their lives and those of their families and friends from the onslaught of the Indians. This symbolism carries the final impact of the drama.

The black world of the play--the preacher and his family and the college students who are participating in a demonstration--is pitted against the white world as represented by the State, the Reverend Phelps, Lyle Britten and his family and friends. But there are some degrees of difference within the two groups. Two black college students wonder why their political activities have to emanate from a church. "I wish

to God I was in an arsenal," Lorenzo says. And
representing the impetuous black young he speaks
about the preacher: "I don't understand Meridian
here. It was his son . . . that got killed,
butchered! Just last week, and yet, here you
sit--in this--this--the house of this damn Almighty God who don't care what happens to nobody,
unless, of course, they're white." That white
God, he complains, has been lynching, burning,
castrating those who were demonstrating against
such age-old practices. And they were sitting
around God's house trying to find ways to refine
God's world. "If I could get my hands on Him,
I'd pull Him out of heaven and drag Him through
this town at the end of a rope," the youth cries.
"No, you wouldn't," Meridian advises and makes
Lorenzo understand that such talk makes him no
better than the whites who attack them. Yet,
Meridian moans, "I cannot rest until they bring
my son's murderer to trial. That man killed my
son." We see here the public and private involvement Meridian feels. He is preparing the
young college students to go out once more and
participate in a non-violent demonstration and
his traditional role as peace-making preacher is
strained.

Meridian believes Parnell James, the white
local newspaper editor, will help. He is a
wealthy liberal who is not economically bound to
whites or blacks. He and Lyle Britten grew up
together from childhood. They are still friends.
He shares with Lyle some of the economic repri-
sal blacks and whites are imposing on the two of
them. Blacks no longer trade at Britten's store
because they know he killed Richard Henry. Parnell has long since lost what little advertise-
ment and subscriptions most whites could give to
his newspaper. They believe he is a foreign
voice among them. They tolerate him because he
is one of them, but they castigate him for his
social leanings. Meridian considers him a
friend because Parnell is the only white man in

town who had advocated doing the right thing for whites and blacks. For the moment, the preacher wants to believe Parnell's sense of ethics would bring about a trial for Lyle. When he mentions this hope to Lorenzo, the young black man tells him he is too trustful. The white man, he says, is a good man only when he wants blacks to be good. Therefore, it is impossible for a black man to ever be bad even if he wants to. "I've got as much right to be bad as anybody else," he claims, and Meridian disagrees on the simple conventional theory, "because you know better."

Meridian slowly moves from the "forgive-them-for-they-know-not-what-they-do" attitude into a far more pragmatic role for a preacher and leader of a black American community--the personality the occasion needs--as the following dialogue with Parnell shows:

Parnell: I hear it was real bad tonight.

Meridian: Not as bad as it's going to get. Maybe I was wrong not to let the people arm.

Parnell: If the Negroes were armed, it's the Negroes who'd be slaughtered. You know that.

Meridian: They're slaughtered anyway. And I don't know that. I thought I knew it-- but now I'm not so sure.

Parnell: What's come over you? What's going to happen to the people in this town, this church--if you go to pieces?

Meridian: Maybe they'll find a leader who can lead them someplace.

Parnell: Somebody with a gun?

(Meridian is silent.)

Is that what you mean?

Meridian: I'm a Christian. I've been a
Christian all my life, like my Mama and
Daddy before me and like their Mama and
Daddy before them. Of course, if you go
back far enough, you get to a point before Christ, if you see what I mean, B.C.--
and at that point, I've been thinking,
black people weren't raised to turn the
other cheek, and in the hope of heaven.
No, then they didn't have to take low.
Before Christ. They walked around just
as good as anybody else, and when they
died, they didn't go to heaven, they went
to join their ancestors. My son's dead,
but he's not gone to join his ancestors.
He was a sinner, so he must have gone to
hell--if we're going to believe what the
Bible says. Is that such an improvement,
such a mighty advance over B.C.? I've
been thinking, I've had to think--would
I have been such a Christian if I hadn't
been born black? Maybe I had to become
a Christian in order to have any dignity
at all. Since I wasn't a man in men's
eyes- then I could be a man in the eyes
of God. But that didn't protect my wife.
She's dead, too soon, we don't really
know how. That didn't protect my son--
he's dead, we know how too well. That
hasn't changed this town--this town, where
you couldn't find a white Christian at
high noon on Sunday! The eyes of God--
maybe those eyes are blind--I never let
myself think of that before.

When Parnell complains that Meridian can't be
the man who gives a signal for a holocaust,
Meridian warms up to his internal struggle by
asking whether he is the man who must watch

while his people are beaten, chained, starved, clubbed, and butchered. Parnell reminds him that he used to say that his people were all the people in the world--all the people God ever made and would make; that his race was the human race. Now Meridian is astonished that one should even use the term "the human race" and Parnell, his liberal friend, is amazed to note "there is something in your tone I've never heard before-- rage--maybe hatred." Meridian answers him crit- ically, "You heard it before. You just never recognized it before. You've heard it in all those blues and spirituals and gospel songs you claim to love so much." As their conversation continues, Meridian expresses the revelation which he has brought himself: that Mr. Charlie can't change. That all white men are Mr. Charlie. Most importantly, at this point he realizes that his friend Parnell Henry is a white man. He too is Mr. Charlie. Continuing the new truth which he and his black friend are now speaking among themselves, Parnell tells Meridian, "You sound more and more like your son, do you know that? A lot of colored people here didn't approve of him, but he said things they had longed to hear, how much he despised white people!" These were not the things he had longed to say to Meridian, corrects Parnell. But the question was not how Richard felt about white people. With Meridian it was that he wanted his son to live and have his own life and that was something Parnell could not understand about being black. To Meridian it was simple: if you are a black man with a black son you have to forget all about white people and concentrate on trying to save your child.

As we have seen Meridian has counted upon his friend Parnell to see to it that a trial is held and that at least the wheels of justice may be set into action as Lyle is brought to answer for the death of Richard. That wish seems small enough but it is large in the particular setting

215

plagued by the attitude toward race Baldwin
wishes to represent. It is further explained as
the dialogue between Parnell and Meridian continues:

> Parnell: That can't have anything to do
> with it, it can't. We must forget about
> all--all the past injustice. We have to
> start from scratch, or do our best to start
> from scratch. It isn't vengeance we're
> after. Is it?

> Meridian: I don't want vengeance. I don't
> want to be paid back--anyway, I couldn't
> be. I just want Lyle to be made to know
> that what he did was evil. I just want
> this town to be forced to face the evil
> that it countenances and turn from evil
> and do good. That's why I've stayed in
> this town so long!

> Parnell: But if Lyle didn't do it? Lyle
> is a friend of mine--a strange friend, but
> a friend. I love him. I know how he suf-
> fers.

> Meridian: How does he suffer?

> Parnell: He suffers--from being in the
> dark--from having things inside him that
> he can't control. He's not a wicked man.
> I know he's not. I've known him almost
> all his life! The face he turns to you,
> Meridian, isn't the face he turns to me.

> Meridian: Is the face he turns to you more
> real than the face he turns to me? You go
> ask him if he killed my son.

> Parnell: They're going to ask him that in
> court. That's why I fought to bring about
> this trial. And he'll say no.

216

Meridian: I don't care what he says in court. You go ask him. If he's your friend, he'll tell you the truth.

Parnell: No. No, he may not. He's-- he's maybe a little afraid of me.

Meridian: If you're his friend, you'll know whether he's telling you the truth or not. Go ask him.

Parnell: I can't do it. I'm his friend. I can't betray him.

Meridian: But you can betray me? You are a white man, aren't you? Just another white man--after all.

Parnell: Even if he says yes, it won't make any difference. The jury will never convict him.

Meridian: Is that why you fought to bring about the trial? I don't care what the jury does. I know he won't say yes to them. He won't say yes to me. But he might say yes to you. You say we don't know. Well, I've got a right to know. And I've got the right to ask you to find out--since your the only man who can find out. And I've got to find out-- whether we've been friends all these years, or whether I've just been your favorite Uncle Tom.

Parnell: You know better than that.

Meridian: I don't know, Parnell, any longer--any of the things I used to know. Maybe I never knew them. I'm tired. Go home.

217

Parnell: You don't trust me anymore,
do you, Meridian?

Meridian: Maybe I never trusted you. I
don't know. Maybe I never trusted myself.
Go home. Leave me alone. I must look
back at my record.

Parnell: Meridian--what you ask I don't
know if I can do it for you.

Meridian: I don't want you to do it for
me. I want you to do it for you. Good
night.

Parnell: Good night.

(Parnell exits. Meridian comes downstage.
It is dawn.)

Meridian: My record! Would God--would
God--would God I had died for thee--my
son, my son!

Further essence of the image of the preacher in Blues comes in contrast between Meridian
and the Reverend Phelps, a pastor in White Town
and a close friend to Lyle Britten and his family. Lyle's wife, Jo, is frightened by the possibility that her husband may be brought to
trial. She cannot understand what has happened
to the black people in town whom she used to
think of as her own people. She cannot recall
ever having known anyone who ever mistreated a
colored person and she certainly does not think
they acted mistreated. Now, however, when she
walks through town she is scared because she does
not know what is going to happen next and she
wonders how colored people learned how to hate
so badly so suddenly. Especially when she and
other whites had given them everything they've
got. Phelps explains to her:

Their minds have been turned. They have
turned away from God. They're a simple
people--warm-hearted and good-natured.
But they are very easily led, and now
they are harkening to the counsel of
these degenerate Communist race-mixers.
And they don't know what terrible harm
they can bring on themselves--and on us
all.

When Parnell James enters Lyle Britten's
home where the friends have gathered to console
the man everyone knows murdered Richard Henry, he
chides Phelps and others who speak scathingly
about communists, going so far as to refer to
Parnell's newspaper as "that communist sheet."
He retorts bitterly: "Ah? But the father of
your faith, the cornerstone of that church of
which you are so precious adornment, was a communist, possibly the first. He may have done
some tom-catting. We know he did some drinking
and he knew a lot of--loose ladies and drunkards.
It's all in the Bible, isn't it, Reverend Phelps?"
The minister refuses to be drawn into Parnell's
blasphemous banter. He simply wants to know
whether Parnell is with them or against them.
Phelps speaks unofficially as the state does of-
ficially, as he laments the possibility that Lyle
may have to stand a trial at all for the murder.
He has talked with the Chief of Police whose hands
are tied by orders from higher up that he has to
actually carry out an arrest and a trial. He has
come to let Lyle know that he and every other
white man in town sympathize with him in his
troubles. Phelp's Christianity considered the
murderer the person who had been aggrieved and
who needed the comfort of his church, rather than
the father of the murder victim. In this manner
the author presents opposing images of the preacher within the Christian religion. Indeed, those
diametrically opposed images tend to reinforce
the plague which Mr. Baldwin felt that Christianity as practiced in the United States represents.

219

When a trial is held, the State frustrates
Meridian's expectation's by placing him, rather
than Lyle on the defensive:

The State:Reverend Henry, you have made
us all aware that your love for your son
transcends your respect for the truth or
your devotion to the church. But--luckily
for the truth--it is a matter of public
record that your son was so dangerously
deranged that it was found necessary for
his own sake, to incarcerate him. It was
at the end of that incarceration that he
returned to this town. We know that his
life in the North was riotous--he brought
that riot into this town. The evidence
is overwhelming. And yet, you, a Christian minister, dare to bring us this tis-
sue of lies in defense of a known pimp,
dope addict, and rapist! You are yourself so eaten up by race hatred that no
word of yours can be believed.

Meridian: Your judgement of myself and
my motives cannot concern me at all. I
have lived with that judgement far too
long. The truth cannot be heard in this
dreadful place. But I will tell you
again what I know. I know why my son
became a dope addict. I know better than
you will ever know, even if I should explain it to you for all eternity, how I
am responsible for that. But I know my
son was not a pimp. He respected women
far too much for that and I know he was
not a rapist. Rape is hard work--and
frankly, I don't think that the alleged
object was my son's type at all!

The State:And you are a minister?

Meridian: I think I may be beginning to
become one.

220

His final image and perhaps the one which
the playwright wishes to be the approved role of
the minister in a society such as that which the
play describes begins to become clear to Meridian
Henry. He must become a different kind of minister than he had been up to this point. His
humiliation on the witness stand shows clearly
the absurdity of his conventional role as the
minister who had used Christianity in the manner
white Americans prescribed for blacks. Lyle,
the murderer of Meridian's son, could say to the
preacher:

> Wasn't much sense in trying me now, this
> time, was there Reverend? These people
> have been knowing me and my good Jo here
> all our lives, they ain't going to doubt
> us. And you people--you people--ought to
> have better sense and more things to do
> than run around stirring up all this hate
> and trouble. That's how your son got him-
> self killed. . . .

Using the last remnants of his conventional
view of the role of the preacher in settings such
as that in which he lives, Meridian believes that
a man-to-man facing between himself and Lyle will
arrive at truth. He asks Lyle, "Did you kill
him?" Lyle answers:

> They just asked me that in court, didn't
> they? And they just decided I didn't,
> didn't they? Well, that's good enough
> for me and all these white people and so
> it damn sure better be good enough for you!

Lyle Britten has been acquitted by the court,
and the State, in its interrogation of Meridian
has left the preacher the culprit. Clearly, the
courts do not dispense justice; they do not respect lives other than those of friends and neighbors of the officers of the court. "I had to
kill him. I'm a white man! Can't nobody talk

221

that way to me" is the only actual defense Lyle Britten needs to give when he speaks to the community. His morality and theirs are one. And, he adds, "I ain't sorry. I want you to know I ain't sorry!"

This is the context in which the people of Black Town make ready to begin their march which they believe now is the only recourse left to them. Their day in court has proved blacks get no worthy hearing of their grievances. Murder of one of theirs is not murder in the eyes of the community, the church, or the courts. This frustration is the efficient cause which radically changes Meridian Henry into a new image of black preacher, as the following dialogue describes it:

> Meridian: You know, for us, it all began with the Bible and the gun. Maybe it will end with the Bible and the gun.
>
> Juanita: What did you do with the gun, Meridian?
>
> Parnell: You have the gun, Richard's gun?
>
> Meridian: Yes. In the pulpit. Under the Bible. Like the pilgrims of old.

A militant church emerges as that which a militant preacher, Meridian Henry, will lead in the future. He has come to that image through the conscious inefficacy of the machinery of the social order that should bring about justice in the community. The play ends with the implication that Meridian Henry, together with a ready-made congregation of the young who already understand the necessity to project themselves as American men and women--not ready victims of the self-image of the Lyle Britten's of the world--will use the Bible and the gun to bring about a

222

proper social order in the nation. This ironic
metaphor, to Baldwin, will eradicate the plague
in Christianity in America. And only the preacher will lead the way. Love, in the traditional
sense, does not exist between the white and black
sectors in "Mr Charlie's" towns in America. So,
the militant church does not expect Christian
love outside its own congregations. Those congregations are either black or white. The
preachers will lead their own respective flocks
toward their social goals, outside Christianity.
Reverend Phelps will comfort the Lyle Britten's;
Reverend Henry will lead the blacks toward justice. Phelps has the courts and majority opin-
ion as the ally for his people; Henry will use
the church and support his movement with the
gun when the Bible fails.

Further, the play's comment on the strength
of economics rings with a bitter clamor. For,
Parnell James, beyond the pale of economic re-
prisal even if boycott is imposed upon him, is
the only white person in the community who can
and does understand the black ambition and need.
At the play's end, he asks Juanita, "Can I join
you on the march, Juanita? Can I walk with you?"
and she answers cryptically, "Well, we can walk
in the same direction, Parnell." Meridian
Henry finds a viable role as preacher to the
community. He remains, however, a preacher without personal love--one whose wife has died mys-
teriously and whose son has been killed by a
society that will not accept him other than in
the self-defacing character America has fashioned for him. This role is limited for Meridian
Henry, but it may well be the only one available
for him for the present.

CHAPTER 9 . . . . MARGARET WALKER'S BROTHER
EZEKIEL: Priest-Prophet of
the "Invisible Church"

> Brother Zeke never talked
> to anybody about his occasion-
> al sallies forth to see the
> world. He was a singing
> preaching man but wasn't much
> for gossip. Sometimes early
> in the morning or about dusk-
> dark a person might spot him
> sitting on the roadside whit-
> tling a stick, or kneeling by
> a creek, or over a small fire
> skinning and cooking catfish
> for his food. He might even
> swap a few words with white
> and black folks alike or be
> humming a tune and whistling
> bird calls, but next thing a
> person knew, the fire was out
> and the man had vanished.

> Margaret Walker, _Jubilee_

Margaret Walker (1915-   ) was born in Birmingham , Alabama, the daughter of university-trained
parents. After having lived in Alabama, Mississippi, and Louisiana in towns which her Methodist
preacher father held pastorates, Walker studied
for a bachelors degree at Northwestern University
which she received in 1935. For the next few
years she worked in Chicago as a typist, newspaper reporter, editor of "little" magazine, member of the staff creative writing program at the
University of Iowa and submitted a collection of
poems for the thesis that led to her masters
degree in 1940. In 1942, her _For My People_ won
the Yale University Younger Poets Competition.
After teaching at Livingston College in North
Carolina, and West Virginia State College, Walker

joined the faculty of Jackson State College in Mississippi. Her novel, Jubilee, was her dissertation for her Ph.D. degree at the University of Iowa. That work won for her a Houghton Mifflin Literary Award in 1966. It has been translated into several languages and has been adapted to musical drama. Walker has written articles for the Yale Review and Saturday Review, among other American publications, and has published individual poems, as well as Prophets for a New Day (1970), a collection of poetry, and How I wrote Jubilee (1972). Her Uncle Ezekial from Jubilee presents the image of the preacher in this study.

Jubilee

Jubilee is the story of the author's maternal grand-mother, through whose eyes and feelings most of the narrative is told with tenderness, objectivity, and authenticity. In the ante-bellum portion, Margaret Walker presents Brother Ezekiel who is not a central character to the plot. He is, however, a clear image of the plantation preacher during slavery, the priest and the prophet of the Afro-American version of Christianity. He plays a complex role in the society as he is the medium for the salvation of the official religion shared by master and slave. He is charismatic. By virtue of his mission and station in the peculiar society he proclaims the conventional doctrine of Christianity; and, at the same time, he forms a new religious community that needs to come into existence to serve the slaves who are brothers and sisters. He preaches the theology and heritage of established Christianity, but his role as priest flies into the face of the society that tolerated him—those who taught him the Bible stories and created his privilege to move from one plantation

226

to another. Brother Ezekiel provides in the novel the meaningful representation of the essence of religion in the destitute lives of the slaves. He embodies the vitality of the "invisible church"; for he serves a multi-purpose role that foreshadows the black preacher and his arcane function in the black church far beyond Emancipation. He is, indeed, an essential feature of Afro-American culture.

Brother Ezekiel's actions and other persons' reactions to what he does come to the novel through the experiences of Vyry, the central character, the slave girl who lives through the beginning of the fall of slavery into the Reconstruction period.

As Jubilee's action begins, Hetta is dying at age 29. She has borne 15 children. John Morris Dutton, "marster" of the plantation, had owned Hetta since she was "barely more than a pickaninny." His father had given him the "nigger wench" when he was a teenager. He sired several of her children, including Vyry, the last one, who he has sent to another plantation to be reared by an elderly slave woman. As Hetta lay dying, Dutton came to the cabin to "look in on her" and to say he has granted her wish to see her last child before she dies.

Brother Ezekiel enters the slave quarter, carrying the child on his shoulders. "Hetta! Hetta! Here is Brother Zeke with Vyry. He done brung your youngun to you," one of the women calls out to the dying woman. Brother Ezekiel holds the child close to her mother's face and says soothingly, "It's your mama, Vyry, say hello to your maw." The child says "Mama," and whimpers as Hetta falls back on her pillow, Ezekiel hands the child back to one of the women and says, "Sis Hetta, I'm here, Brother Zeke, it's me. Can I do something for you?" When she asks him to pray, he immediately falls to his knees

227

beside the bed, takes the dying woman's hand into his, and begins to pray:

> Lord, God-a-mighty, you done told us in
> your Word to seek and we shall find; knock
> and the door be open; ask, and it shall
> be given when your love come twinklin down.
> And Lord, tonight we is a-seekin. Way
> down here in this here rain-washed world,
> kneelin here by this bed of affliction
> pain, your humble servant is a-knockin,
> and askin for your lovin mercy, and your
> tender love. This here sister is tired
> a-sufferin, Lord, and she wants to come
> on home. We ask you to roll down that
> sweet chariot right here by her bed, just
> like you done for Lishy, so she can step
> in kinda easy like and ride on home to
> glory. Gather her in your bosom like you
> done Father Abraham and give her rest.
> She weak, Lord, and she weary, but her
> eyes is a-fixin for to light on them gold-
> en streets of glory and them pearly gates
> of God. She beggin for to set at your
> welcome table and feast on milk and honey.
> She wants to put on them angel wings and
> wear that crown and them pretty little
> golden slippers. She done been broke like
> a straw in the wind and she ain't got no
> strength, but she got the faith, Lord, and
> she got the promise of your Almighty Word.
> Lead her through this wilderness of sin
> and tribulation. Give her grace to stand
> by the river of Jordan and cross her over
> to hear Gabe blow that horn. Take her
> home, Lord God, take her home.

The women standing around the bed sobbed and breathed fervent "amens." Brother Ezekiel got up from his knees and covered Hetta's hands with the bedspread. She was dead now, and he had performed the last rites of the religion for her and the mourners. As a priest of Christianity he has

represented his religion at the time of the
death of one of his parishioners. He has expressed the cornerstone of his faith that is a
life after that brings surcease from suffering
for the faithful. As poet of his people, he has
articulated the theology of death and resurrection in terms of the "sweet chariot," the "golden
streets of glory," "the pearly gates," the "welcome table," the "feast on milk and honey," the
"angel wings," and the "pretty little golden
slippers." These images permeate the Negro
spirituals and the poetry the black preacher
uses in his sermons and prayers. It is appropriate language for the occasion. It abounds in
imagery, but refers to slavery only obliquely.
The prayer for the dead is one artifact in the
continuum of the preacher's art and his role.

As priest and prophet of the "invisible
church," Ezekiel conducted religious services at
the Rising Glory Baptist Church, deep in the
swamps and a long way from the Big House. Here,
in the privacy of their own domain, the slave
society creates its own world and expresses its
own aspirations. Through Vyry's percetpions,
the reader learns how important the church in
the swamps was to the slaves. No matter how
tired Aunt Sally, the woman who had the responsibility for rearing Vyry, became the work day,
she never failed on Big Meeting Nights to go
hear Brother Ezekiel preach. Together with
Aunt Sally, the little girl walked a great distance across the plantation to the church, but
she was always excited with the prospect of
hearing the preaching and joining in the singing. The songs were wonderful and spirited,
and learning them became a delight to the child
during the intervals between Big Meetings, as
she sang "Steal Away," and "I Got Shoes" and
"I'm Goin' to Sit at the Welcome Table" and "The
Old Sheep Knows the Road." Brother Ezekiel almost always chose his text from the great leaders
of the Hebrew people: the prophets, the kings,

the judges, and the men whom God had used to lead his people. His favorite and most prominent figure was Moses and the story of his leading the children of Israel out of Egypt, out of the House of Bondage, to a vision of the Promised Land. It represented an acceptable syncretization of conventional Christian homily and slave aspirations. And it provided broad opportunities for religious frenzy. Indeed, it was one of the most popular Bible stories preached at the Rising Glory Baptist Church.

Jubilee provides a meaningful sermon scene which illustrates this politico-religious purpose of the preacher as this performance, together with his congregation, illustrates:

"They was ordered by the king to make bricks out of straw."

"Oh, yeah."

"And then they was commanded to make bricks out of nothing."

"Oh, yeah."

"Hear me this evening, children. They made the Hebrew children bend beneath the lash."

"Oh, yeah."

"And they ordered the midwives to kill the new-born boychild in the birthing pots."

"Oh, yeah."

"Well now, listen to me. God didn't like it. No siree! He didn't like it one little bit. No siree!"

"And he let it go on just as long as he
was able to stand it. And then he say
he can't stand it no more. And Moses was
born to some poor persecuted Hebrew
slaves."

"Yes, he was."

"And his mammy saved him and hid him for
three months. Yes, she did, bless God,
cause she knowed God had him for a purpose.
And she made a little basket and stuck
him in the swampy water where the king's
daughter come to bathe in the cool of the
evening. And listen to me preaching this
evening. I wants to tell you she took him
in the Big House, yes she done it, she
done that very thing. She took him in
Pharoah's house, that cruel slave owner
what was persecuting God's children, what
God didn't like, what God didn't have to
stand. And God seen fit to use Moses,
yes, he sho-nuff used him. And when he
called him he said, 'Son, I wants you to
go down yonder and tell that cruel hard-
hearted slave marster to let my peoples
go. And tell him I won't take "No" for an
answer. Tell him I say I done run clean
outen patience. And you tell him I am the
God what Am and Always was and Always will
Be. And I'm gettin awful tired of his
foolishness. Tell him all I gotta do is
snap my fingers and he won't have no water
to drink. And all I gotta do is stretch
out my rod over the land and make suffering
the bedfellow of every living man. I can
heal the pain and can kill the sorrow. You
tell him I say be quick about it. And let
my peoples go.'"

As the biblical story ended, Brother
Ezekiel's voice would soften to a whisper, even
deep in the swamp and far from the Big House, as

he admonished his flock to have faith in God who would send them a Moses, a deliverer to free His people and prove to the world what the Bible says about a servant being worthy of his hire. Vyry began to understand that the delight found in listening to the sermon and in joining in the singing was only a part of the activity of the Rising Glory Baptist Church. She learned eventually that these meetings served a double purpose, and Aunt Sally punctuated the wonderment with the mysterious promise that when she was older and had her "womanhood" she could be baptized by Brother Ezekiel. She learned quickly that nobody must mention a word of the sermons to the white folks, even under the pain of death; for white folks were naturally mean and could not help themselves anyhow.

Another purpose of the church, the preacher, and the congregation of slaves is illustrated in the novel, again through the eyes of the young Vyry, when Aunt Sally asks the master for a pass through town to go to his other plantation on Sunday. She said she was going to visit a sick cousin, and John Dutton, who considered himself a good slave owner, agreed that she should have a pass. Vyry thought they were going to church to hear Brother Ezekiel preach about God and the Hebrew children and the Moses who was going to set them free. But she sensed through Aunt Sally's seriousness that they were not going to attend an ordinary Sunday meeting. Aunt Sally's Sam, Big Boy, and some other slaves from the other plantations were there. They were reading and explaining some papers to the slaves. Illiterate slaves, including Aunt Sally, were learning of the new laws and revisions in the Black Code tightening the control of master over slave. They had been smuggled into Georgia and were in the hands of slaves on John Dutton's plantations. In these years, leading up to the Civil War, tensions were rampant, and Georgia law forbade a slave or a free black to handle in his hands a

232

a piece of paper, pencil, pen, writing papers, books, magazines or any printed materials.

His mobility throughout the countryside was most important to his function as Brother Ezekiel used his ingenuity to carry out his complex role as preacher to the slaves on the two Dutton plantations. He hid from potentially hostile white men, sometimes assuming the role of scarecrow. Most times he came and went unnoticed, indicating the importance slaveowners gave to his position as preacher and indicating their total ignorance of his role as conductor along the Underground Railroad. He could write his own passes, but his master did not know that. "This nigger preacher belongs to me. He has my consent to go to town and visit his sick nigras on my place," Brother Ezekiel usually wrote for himself, signing J.M. Dutton's name. Most times he did not have to show the pass, but he kept it on his person for emergencies. Traveling in the early morning or late at night from one plantation to another, through the swamp woods and up the river branches, nobody took notice of him since he seemed to belong to everybody and everywhere. Most times he was alone, but often he was accompanied by some other slave who may be escaping from slavery or going to visit a family member. As Jubilee explains simply, Brother Zeke never talked to anybody about his occasional sallies forth to see the world. He was a singing and preaching man but wasn't much for gossip. Sometimes early in the morning or about dusk-dark a person might spot him sitting on a roadside whittling a stick, or kneeling by a creek, or over a small fire skinning and cooking a catfish for his food. He might even swap a few words with white and black alike, or he could be found humming a tune or whistling bird calls. Before anyone knew it, the fire was out and the preacher had moved on. He was especially kind to the sick. He told funny stories to sick children, explained things to them that nobody else would bother to tell them, and always shared his wealth of Bible stories.

Brother Ezekiel's image as the preacher stands out in bold relief in Jubilee's scene on a July Fourth celebration when all of the slaves and everyone else on the plantation was carried to town to witness the patriotic festivities, carried out alongside the hanging of some slaves who had been convicted for inciting a rebellion on the master's plantation. Young Vyry heard a white preacher take his text from "the Fourth Book of Moses" and preach on the subject MURDER. "Whoso killeth any person, the murderer shall be put to death," he thundered to his audience, and claimed that those were the eternal words of God and that God cannot lie. In directing a part of his sermon to the planters who were masters of the African slaves, he exclaimed:

> My friends, I speak to you leading farmers of Lee County as your humble servant. I admonish you in the name of the Lord and fear of God to guard your property with your lives! Remember your slaves are your sacred property. They are committed to you as a sacred trust from God. Read in His Holy Word where he tells you that your bondservants are yours and you are responsible for them. You are morally obligated to teach them right from wrong. You must constantly tell them the awful consequences of evil doing and the heavenly rewards for obedience and faithful service. God does everything well and for a purpose. Since the beginning of civilized man there have been slaves and masters and there always will be. Slavery is a natural and righteous state. It is the civilizing principle of all great societies. Yours is the God-given right to admonish your slave in the fear of the Lord; to punish him when he does wrong and to teach him of the

234

heavenly rewards after death that God
has in store for him when he is your
faithful, humble, and obedient servant.
The Christianizing of the black heathen
is your sacred duty. He was brought to
these great shores for a Christian purpose. It is your duty so see that that
great and sacred purpose is fulfilled;
that the savage becomes a docile, faithful, humble and obedient servant.

That portion of his sermon was far different
from Brother Ezekiel's and it took no cognizance
of the double purposes for which the Rising
Glory Baptist Church met as often as was feasi-
ble. Surely, his admonition to the slaves, a
second part of his sermon, was equally as foreign to Vyry whose religion had been nurtured in
the brush-arbor of Brother Ezekiel's church, as
he continued:

And, now, I turn to you black slaves. You
are fortunate to have found Christian
masters and to be cared for by these wonderful gentlemen. They protect and feed
and clothe and shelter you. You must
reward them with faithful service and
strict obedience. You must obey the law
of Moses when he says, Thou shalt not kill,
thou shalt not steal, thou shalt not lie!
Do you know what these commandments mean?
Do you know what will happen when you kill,
when you steal, and when you lie? I will
tell you. God says He is a God who will
never forget the disobedient. He will
punish you and your children and your
children's children, all your little
black pickaninnies down to the third and
fourth generations, but He will have mercy on them that keep his commandments and
obey Him.

Not a slave changed his expression. No one

235

was impressed with the fire and brimstone of the white preacher's sermon. He simply was not preaching about the same Moses and the same God that held so important a position at Rising Glory Baptist Church. Their own circumstances caused them to practice and to believe in a kind of "cultural religion" which they fashioned for themselves out of the stories of God and Moses. When their sermons were filtered through their own cultural valve--their own identification with suffering and their own sense of hope for freedom--the practice of their religion became unique, powerful, meaningful, and quickly infused into the consciousness and value system of the entire slave community. Excerpts from the white preacher's sermon show the Christian religion provided slave and master a diametrical opposite personal application to their own circumstances.

This image of the black preacher in Jubilee projects a personality and a practice unlike any other requirement for the Christian ministry in the nation. By the middle of the 19th century, a priesthood had developed among the slaves which was pointed already toward the complex and powerful role which the preacher was to play in the Black American experience through the Civil War, Reconstruction, and into the present day. Unlike any of his counterparts among other ethnic groups, the history of Afro-Americans placed demands upon the preacher which are at once glorious and frightening. It is a most positive image, even if an almost impossible one to be realized by men. Jubilee shows in Brother Ezekiel the self-sacrificing, miracle-working minister to the hopeless and the frightened, the source of vital information, and the chief politician of his entire society. Although that image has been modified to some extent in the years since the abolition of slavery, its roots were founded deeply in a time and a society in which that pattern was indispensible.

Even in conscious art, Margaret Walker
sought to preserve the folk quality of the ante-
bellum black society to permeate her novel. The
role of the preacher in that setting and his
socio-political responsibility may be seen in
Professor Walker's own words taken from her "How
I Wrote Jubilee":

> I always intended Jubilee to be a folk
> novel based on folk material: folk say-
> ings, folk belief, folkways. As early as
> 1948 I was conceiving the story in terms
> of this folklore. I also wanted the book
> to be realistic and humanistic. I intended
> this twin standard to prevail, and I wanted
> as well to press the leit-motif of the
> biblical analogy of Hebrews in Egypt with
> black folk in America. I had always known
> that Negro slaves prayed for a Moses to
> deliver them from Pharoah. For instance,
> Brother Ezekiel is in the tradition of the
> slave preacher who was conductor on the
> Underground Railroad, who preached of our
> deliverance through a God-sent Moses, and
> who also served as a spy in the Union
> Army, doing all he could toward gaining
> freedom. In Reconstruction, Vyry echoes
> this theme when she says she knows people
> must wander a while in the wilderness.
> Like all freed slaves they believed they
> were on their way to the Promised Land.

After Emancipation, the slave preacher's
influence could be felt strongly by those freed-
men who, in the wake of the Union Army's advances
through the South, caused the strongest possible
socio-religious institutions to be established
there--their churches and their church-related
schools. How effectively Brother Ezekiel's
ministry influenced the personal lives of those
for whom his type served as spiritual leader may
be seen in that portion of Jubilee which describes Vyry's turn to her inner resources in a

serious fight which threatened to destroy her family in Reconstruction. The scene illustrates a touching religious experience aside from the necessities of the "invisible church"—one transcending the multi-purpose urgencies of the utility of a black religion and falling solidly into the highest tradition of a personal religion, even if it has been learned deep in the forest, far from the plantation owner who taught Christianity to his slaves:

Before she realized where she was going she found herself deep in the woods. Around her there was a chapel-hush. She heard birds softly and sweetly singing, but most of all she felt the silence of the thickly soft carpet of pine needles under her feet, and looking up she could faintly see the blue sky in thin scraps of light through the interlacing of tender young leaves and green pine needles. She found herself a rock, and instead of sitting down she dropped to her knees. Instinctively she began to pray, the words forming on her lips at first in a halting, faltering, and half-hesitant fashion, and then rushing out: "Lawd, God-a-mighty, I come down here this morning to tell you I done reached the end of my rope, and I wants you to take a-hold. I done come to the bottom of the well, Lord, and my well full of water done run clean dry

"I come down here, Lord, cause I ain't got no where else to go. I come down here knowing I ain't got no right, but I got a heavy need. I'm suffering so. Lord, my body is heavy like I'm carrying a stone. I come to ask you to move the stone, Jesus. Please move the stone! I come down here, Lord, to ask you to come by here, Lord. Please come by here!

"We can't go on like this no longer,
Lord. We can't keep on a-fighting, and
a-fussing, and a-cussing, and a-hating
like this, Lord. You done been too good
to us. We done wrong. Lord, I knows we
done wrong. I ain't gwine say we ain't
done wrong, and I ain't gwine promise we
might not do wrong again cause, Lord, we
ain't nothing but sinful human flesh, we
ain't nothing but dust. We is evil peoples
in a wicked world, but I'm asking you to
let your forgiving love cover our sin,
Lord.

"Let your peace come in our hearts
again, Lord, and we's gwine try to stay
on our knees and follow the road You is
laid before us, if You only will.

"Come by here, Lord, come by here, if
you please. And Lord, I wants to thank
You, Jesus, for moving the stone!"

Now with the morning rocking around her
like a storm shaking through the earth
beneath her, she waited till the thundering sound of crashing trees and trembling
worlds had ceased, and she got up from her
knees. She looked around, startled and
almost amazed that the day was still so
hushed and still. The sunlight dappled
through the trees and she put her hands
out to touch the absolutely motionless
leaves. In wonder she looked again at the
blue sky, and then in a sudden lightness
of movement, feeling that once again she
was a feather, she began to pick her way
out of the woods. She touched her wet
cheeks with one exploring finger and,
drying them on her apron, she spoke aloud,
"My eyes must be red and I must look a
sight. I reckon I better wash my face in
the brook before I goes back to the house."

Walter C. Daniel--Professor of English, University of Missouri-Columbia, has taught public school in Los Angeles, California, South Dakota, Ohio, North Carolina and Missouri. He has served as English Department Head and Humanities Division Chairman at Saint Augustine's College, Raleigh, North Carolina, and at North Carolina State Agricultural and Technical University, Greensboro, North Carolina. He has served as President of Lincoln University of Missouri, and as Vice Chancellor at the University of Missouri-Columbia. He holds bachelors, masters and doctors degrees in English and has studied higher education business management at the Harvard University Graduate School of Business. His articles on modern drama and Afro-American literature have appeared in American periodicals, including, The Bulletin of the New York Public Library, College Language Association Journal, Journal of Popular Culture, Crisis, Missouri Historical Review, and Bulletin of Negro History.